Millionaire Success Habits

A Real Way to Financial Independence

(Mastering the Skills of Top Performers to Build Happiness, Wealth & Freedom)

Willard Irvin

Published By **Regina Loviusher**

Willard Irvin

All Rights Reserved

Millionaire Success Habits: A Real Way to Financial Independence (Mastering the Skills of Top Performers to Build Happiness, Wealth & Freedom)

ISBN 978-0-9958659-2-1

No part of this guidebook shall be reproduced in any form without permission in writing from the publisher except in the case of brief quotations embodied in critical articles or reviews.

Legal & Disclaimer

The information contained in this ebook is not designed to replace or take the place of any form of medicine or professional medical advice. The information in this ebook has been provided for educational & entertainment purposes only.

The information contained in this book has been compiled from sources deemed reliable, and it is accurate to the best of the Author's knowledge; however, the Author cannot guarantee its accuracy and validity and cannot be held liable for any errors or omissions. Changes are periodically made to this book. You must consult your doctor or get professional medical advice before using any of the suggested remedies, techniques, or information in this book.

Upon using the information contained in this book, you agree to hold harmless the Author from and against any damages, costs, and expenses, including any legal fees potentially resulting from the application of any of the information provided by this guide. This disclaimer applies to any damages or injury caused by the use and application, whether directly or indirectly, of any advice or information presented, whether for breach of contract, tort, negligence, personal injury, criminal intent, or under any other cause of action.

You agree to accept all risks of using the information presented inside this book. You need to consult a professional medical practitioner in order to ensure you are both able and healthy enough to participate in this program.

Table Of Contents

Chapter 1: Creating A Millionaire 1

Chapter 2: Habits Of Millionaires And Billionaires 30

Chapter 3: Types Of Income 55

Chapter 4: Take Advantage Of The Internet 70

Chapter 5: The Power Of Your Team 81

Chapter 6: The Wonder Of The Worldview 97

Chapter 7: You Are Your Own Hero 135

Chapter 8: Mornings To Mega-Mornings 173

Chapter 1: Creating A Millionaire

"Before you may turn out to be a millionaire, you have to learn to think like one. You ought to discover ways to motivate your self to counter fear with courage. Making important choices about your career, commercial enterprise, investments and different sources conjures up fear, fear this is part of the method of becoming a monetary success."

- Thomas J. Stanley

From a poor person's attitude there's only one element that is going into developing a millionaire: money. People who do no longer have money accept as true with that the simplest aspect this is required to make a person rich is cash. While money is what creates the definition of rich, it simply isn't the best detail required in without a doubt creating a millionaire. If you want to turn out to be a millionaire, you ought to examine all of the steps that simply pass into becoming one.

Emphasize On What You Need to Know

Education is a pain factor for plenty folks who are looking for to become a millionaire. They both sink tens of hundreds of bucks into an academic degree that best serves them in a single way, or they complain that they don't have enough schooling to make cash. The reality is that a huge majority of the individuals who are millionaires are not knowledgeable about their businesses thru an actual training or university degree.

In truth, the best millionaires are folks that chose the sector they desired to get into and then invested their time studying what they needed to realize a good way to be triumphant. Those who spend large quantities of time and money gaining more information than they'll ever require to succeed will conflict to be triumphant ultimately. Massive quantities of debt can lead to economic inadequacy and now and again being over knowledgeable can lead to a whole new realm of problems, along with feeling entitled. While this isn't always continually the case and there are numerous graduates who will obtain success, it's far vital that you don't emphasize on your success totally on what you have found out. Instead, pay attention to what you recognize about the industry you're stepping into and emphasize on that.

When you spend an excessive amount of time studying approximately each unmarried aspect below a specific industry, you waste valuable time that could have been spent mastering approximately what sincerely matters. The fact is that only a certain amount of knowledge is required that allows you to get through the stairs and get to where you want to go. Emphasize on what you do realize, and ensure which you invest a while in studying what is surely vital in preference to looking to research each single element about any given subject matter.

Be Willing to Sacrifice

No millionaire ever executed their fame via sitting around gambling video video games or partying each day. If you want to become a millionaire you want to be willing to make sacrifices. People who are not willing to sacrifice their leisure time in prefer of earning profits are not going to grow to be millionaires. While it is vital to have entertainment time and revel in your existence, it's also vital which you spend a sizeable quantity of time invested in creating your economic wealth.

Smart millionaires are ones who schedule time for fun and have interaction in nothing however amusing for the duration of that time. They shut off their telephones, tune out distractions, and absolutely make investments inside the interest they may be carrying out. When they do that, they provide themselves the opportunity to let out and revel in existence itself. That way while they may be finished they can return their complete focus to their goals and retain operating in the direction of the money. Even when you are having fun, you want to take into account of what you are doing. You in no way want to start spending too much cash in your amusing as you may become depleting your financial savings and you may in no way turn out to be a millionaire.

When it comes to certainly getting things performed, you need to be willing to make sacrifices to live centered. The system of becoming a millionaire can become lonely. While all your buddies are out buying modern-day element, partying, and doing other wonderful matters you're going to need to be centered on earning your wealth. If you could do this, then you are certain which will reap millionaire fame.

Accept Defeat and Mistakes

Millionaires recognise the way to accept defeat and errors. They can recognize when some thing was achieved incorrect or hasn't gone their manner and they could take delivery of it. Because in their capacity to just accept it they could circulate on and use it as a lesson to leverage them into greater achievement going forward. A millionaire in no way dwells on defeat or mistakes that they have experienced in their lifetime, no matter the magnitude.

Learning to let pass of errors and defeats is a obligatory a part of being capable of have a millionaire mindset. If you want to acquire millionaire popularity to your lifetime you want to accept the reality that you are going to bear many instances of defeat and mistakes. The reality is that there's truly no manner which will end up a millionaire without making mistakes and being defeat at some points. Being a millionaire means being able to adapt with lifestyles and make selections based totally on what happens to you and around you. If you're making a mistake or are defeat in besides, you need to simply accept it, understand the cutting-edge state of affairs, and make the necessary adjustments so you can hold working towards your fulfillment.

Aim Higher

If you want to attain millionaire reputation you need to purpose higher than 1,000,000. Your universal goal have to be to make 1,000,000, and your long-term purpose need to be to make lots greater. Millionaires recognize the significance of their desires and that they work in the direction of achieving the ones dreams on a regular foundation. Millionaires don't only set realistic dreams, they set large desires. The more you got down to achieve, the harder you will work to acquire that.

When you are placing the purpose to be a millionaire, set the aim to be a rich person. That way, you can have something big to paintings in the direction of. Also, once you gain your first million you'll be prepared to work harder to reap your second, third, fourth, 5th and all subsequent hundreds of thousands. Always set your goals appreciably better than you initially set out to attain, knowing that the larger you dream, the more you reap.

Be Honest

A millionaire who makes one million greenbacks by using being a liar is a millionaire who will never maintain his fame. Once your popularity is tarnished, no person will put money into you. You will now not be capable of get companions, nobody will need to spend money on your products, services, or organisation, and you may now not be capable of earn large income degrees. You should understand that one foremost dent into your popularity can damage your reputation for life. Companies who are exposed for being dishonest can never regain their recognition, despite the fact that they absolutely clean it and work toward the betterment of their popularity for the relaxation of their days in enterprise.

Your reputation is critical to your capacity to turn out to be a millionaire. You ought to examine the importance of your recognition and hold it by means of being honest and staying authentic on your word. A millionaire who stays proper to their word is a millionaire who will be able to preserve their repute and amplify their profits even greater unexpectedly than before.

Stop Limiting Yourself

People can restriction themselves in an limitless variety of methods. Poor mindset, bad behavior, and a lack of private improvement can all lead to you limiting your capability to obtain achievement. If you need to emerge as a millionaire the best aspect you can do is understand your obstacles after which take motion to dispose of them. Any limits you put on yourself are going to be infinitely greater adverse than any limits that ever may be positioned upon you by means of society or other outside affects.

In this ebook you're going to analyze the cost of your mind-set and what you may do to stop proscribing yourself and open yourself up to achieving some thing you preference. The greater you figure in the direction of your non-public development and working thru those barriers, the in addition you are going a good way to pass in phrases of achieving your millionaire status.

Millionaires recognize that their reputation is achieved by means of a lot more than simply money. It entails a cautious balance of personal improvement, willpower, and resolution. Without these elements there's definitely no manner to emerge as a millionaire. If you need to become a millionaire the primary component you must do is find out about all that is going into turning into one after which prepare yourself to turn out to be that person. When you stay congruent with the manner a true millionaire lives then you definitely have the best possibility to grow to be a millionaire for your very own existence. Once you find out about all that goes into developing a millionaire you can begin mirroring those behavior and sports on your very own life and then you may see predominant improvements toward you becoming a millionaire your self.

Millionaire Mindset

"I used to define success as being capable of produce any outcomes you wanted, whether or not it turned into a dating, weightloss, being a millionaire, impacting the lifestyle, changing society, whatever it might be - it is probably homelessness, some thing. Lately, I've redefined fulfillment as 'fulfilling your souls motive'."

- Jack Canfield

Millionaires gain their status by using expertise the significance of mind-set. If you ask any millionaire approximately their mindset styles you may study that they may be very strict about how they consider lifestyles and the sector round them. They do not allow for themselves to foster poor mind-set behavior due to the fact they recognize how detrimental those may be in the direction of their total fulfillment. If a millionaire desires to make millions, they ought to be primed so that it will achieve this. They can top themselves by way of gaining knowledge of their mind-set and spotting the power in their thoughts as a tool in leveraging them in the direction of making the tens of millions they preference.

If you need to come to be a millionaire you need to apprehend the significance of your thoughts and how your mind-set patterns and behaviors can affect your fulfillment. Being capable of succeed comes from extraordinary discipline, an ability to govern your thoughts effectively, and excessive emotional intelligence. Not one millionaire capabilities a low stage of emotional intelligence. If they do, they may not maintain their fame for an extended time frame and therefore they need to no longer be taken into consideration an idol or function version.

There are many precise ways that millionaires use their mindset as a device to reap fulfillment. In order for you to gain fulfillment you must apprehend and make use of these methods to acquire your success. The following mindset behaviors and styles are ones which you want to embody in case you are going to turn out to be a millionaire. Give your self good enough time to actually combine each of these patterns into your lifestyles so you can honestly benefit maximum benefit from them. Recognize that these need to be permanent lifestyle changes. If you deal with these like a section or a fad, you are not going to benefit lasting advantages from them.

Live Within' Your Means

People who are rich understand what it way to live inside' their manner and that they do it. People who're rich do not get there by way of burning through their life financial savings and spending the whole thing they have got in lifestyles. Instead, they apprehend their internet really worth and they live within' their manner. Because of this sort of modesty, they may be capable of boom their way rapidly over time. Even as soon as a wealthy character turns into millionaire, rich person or billionaire, they'll nonetheless search for excellent offers and bargains. Wealthy humans nearly in no way pay full-charge for something, and if they do it's because it is really worth the investment. They are able to recognize the importance of cash and they searching for to spend it inside the great feasible methods.

Never Gamble

Wealthy people don't gamble. Did you recognize that seventy seven% of folks who conflict financially play the lottery on a everyday foundation? This is due to the fact they don't recognize what genuinely is going into creating financial wealth and so they are trying to find to make rapid money this manner. The fact is, they may probably by no means win it. Rich humans want to know where their money goes and they fee odds which are of their choose. Knowing how poorly the chances are stacked within the lottery method that it's a no-brainer that they gained't gamble in any respect. It certainly isn't worth it. Rich humans want to put money into method that get results, now not hazard.

Read Daily

88% of rich humans read for half-hour or more every unmarried day. Reading offers you the possibility to analyze extra, to engage in private development, and to enlarge your mind. You can analyze an limitless quantity of expertise via regular reading. If you want to be a millionaire, you must embrace studying. There is understanding within' written text that you virtually can't discover anywhere else. Ideally, you should are looking for to examine a ebook every week. The more you examine, the better. Always set apart time for studying on a day by day basis.

Spend Less Time in Front of Screens

People who spend their time in front of screens on a everyday basis are not effective. There are records that show that -thirds of all of the wealthy human beings within the global watch TV for less than an hour consistent with day, rather seventy seven% of those who are suffering financially spend an hour or extra watching TV on a daily basis. 74% or extra of those who are suffering financially spend one or extra hour every day using the Internet recreationally. If you need to be a millionaire, you need to reduce out the distractions that come with regular screen time. While there's nothing wrong with the usage of the net or watching TV, you want to be organized to reduce your display time so you can invest a while into activities that will simply get you consequences.

Control Your Emotions

People who are incapable of controlling their emotions will conflict to attain achievement in existence. A loss of control over your feelings can result in you saying stuff you remorse, making choices you remorse, and ultimately sabotaging your very own capability to succeed in existence. Instead of self-sabotaging in this way, learn to increase your emotional intelligence. The more you may perceive and manipulate your emotions, the less complicated it will be with the intention to grasp your attitude and establish healthful behaviors so that it will will let you be more effective in life. Never let your emotions manage you, discover ways to manipulate your emotions.

Network and Volunteer on A Regular Basis

There is a top notch quantity of value that comes from networking and volunteering on a ordinary foundation. When you are engaged in sports simplest for the income, human beings will start to believe that you are not actual. You may also war to come to be known or observed by using other people. If you want to come to be visible and diagnosed, you need to network and volunteer on a normal basis. This builds a high quality recognition for your self, and it additionally increases the quantity of visibility you advantage. You never recognise who you will meet when you attend ordinary occasions without the aim of making business deals and creating wealth.

Work Hard

Rich humans don't get wealthy via being lazy and working minimum hours. If you want to be wealthy, you need to paintings difficult. Wake up, show up, and live as lengthy because it takes to make every day a achievement. Those who awaken late, arrive overdue, and depart early in desire of having a laugh are in no way going to make a millionaire life-style. Instead, they may be going to conflict with their finances all the time. While it's miles crucial which you play tough whilst it's time for play, you should additionally be operating hard when it's time to work. Make positive which you paintings two times as tough than you play so that after it comes time to play you may completely let loose and not worry that you are dropping more money than you are incomes at some stage in your amusement time.

Set Goals

A millionaire by no means works toward "something". They work towards "the thing". They by no means wing it: they set dreams and that they achieve them. There is no price in running toward an unidentified aim. You will by no means feel encouraged to reap it and consequently you may in no way attain some thing in existence. Instead, you will go similarly backwards than you would have in case you had genuinely set desires. Your dreams should vary in size and period. You should have long-time period desires which are going to serve you ultimately and also you ought to have shorter desires that you may swiftly accomplish. Accomplishing shorter desires on a ordinary foundation will come up with the confidence and momentum you want to retain operating closer to the bigger goals.

Never Procrastinate

Procrastinating is a habit this is fostered by way of folks that do not acquire achievement in existence. If you need to be successful, you want to ditch the addiction of procrastination and work toward goals on a everyday foundation. Even the uncomfortable, unenjoyable and difficult tasks have to be performed in a well timed manner. If you procrastinate, you will never attain what you want to in order to be triumphant at becoming a millionaire. Make a address your self that any time you have got a tough or unenjoyable project that wishes to be executed, you will do it first earlier than some other duties. That manner, it's far completely out of the manner and you do now not should worry approximately it to any extent further. It will reduce pressure, boom productivity, and go away you freedom on your time table to accomplish whatever you need to acquire.

Talk Less, Listen More

Nothing can be received with the aid of spending too much time talking and now not sufficient time listening. It is treasured to research whilst it is a great time to talk and while you should be quiet and listen. Those who concentrate learn a awesome deal of records, gain attitude on life, and open up their possibilities. People like to be heard, so being able to listen successfully will permit people to feel heard and valued in existence. This method that the crucial individuals who can contribute toward your success will revel in speaking to you. They can be extra inclined to teach you, and assist you acquire fulfillment on your lifestyles. You need to be coachable and you need to be inclined to pay attention.

Avoid Toxic Relationships

Toxic relationships have a harmful effect on everybody worried. They can affect you in methods a good way to have devastating results toward your ability to acquire fulfillment in lifestyles. If you want to be a success, you want to be inclined to reduce ties with toxic relationships and handiest welcome positive and productive relationships into your life. People who get caught in poisonous relationships can swiftly go to pot their emotions of self esteem, their self-esteem, and their self-self belief. They fail to obtain their dreams due to the fact they start to trust that their dreams are not viable. If you want to be successful, you need to stop having relationships with toxic humans. Consider this: you are the sum of the five people you spend maximum of some time with. If you're spending time with degree ones and twos, maybe even a few stage threes, you are never going to advance to stage four or 5 wealth. You ought to be aware over the human beings you spend a while with and spend time handiest with those who are as dedicated to success as you are.

Don't Give Up

You are going to listen "no" and other shut downs on a regular basis. This is genuine in lifestyles and in business. If you are not prepared to hear these rejections, you want to do some thing you could to put together yourself. You are by no means going to get a straight-shot possibility with none resistance, setbacks, defeats, errors, failures, or different limitations on the way to preserve you lower back for a time period. If you want to be successful, you need to be prepared to maintain persevering toward your desires in spite of these resistances. Never surrender, maintain your dreams in sight and usually paintings closer to them. The extra you work towards your desires, the much more likely you're going to gain them. If you need to be a millionaire, you need to in no way give up to your goals.

Ditch Limiting Beliefs

"I am not worth", "I am not enough", "Success isn't for me", "I am not lucky", and other phrases are highly limiting in what they let you believe approximately your self. If you constantly dumb yourself down in your beliefs, you're by no means going to reap success in your existence. You have to be prepared to ditch your limiting ideals and start questioning high-quality mind. Whenever a proscribing notion enters your mind you ought to take some time to identify it after which remove it. When you do this successfully, you may be capable of release the limiting ideals and open up the possibility so one can make bigger your options. You are best as small as you watched you are. If you want to be bigger than you are, suppose bigger than you are. It is that easy.

Make Your Own Luck

People who wait for luck are individuals who play the lottery and assume to win it. It may additionally manifest, but the odds are not right enough to bet on. If you want to be a millionaire, you have to make your very own luck. Develop positive habits, paintings for your personal improvement, apprehend your bad behaviors and put off them, search for possibilities pursue bonuses, new corporations and appropriate fitness, and do the whole thing within' your control to strengthen yourself through lifestyles. There is no price in watching for the luck of the draw to fall into your lap. If you need to succeed in life, you have to make your own luck and pave the way in your very own achievement.

Know Your Purpose

It is critical that you apprehend what your motive is in existence. People who pursue cash believing that riches is their reason are the same type of folks who emerge as rich and devastated. If you need to revel in your lifestyles, you need to become aware of what your cause is and paintings in alignment along with your life's reason. Pursue your lifelong dream and also you becomes the wealthier and happiest of the people in the international. However, pursue riches without any aim to discover or pursue your reason and you'll be one of the poorest within the global. If you don't recognize what your cause is, your first actual challenge is to discover.

Adapt to Change

The final aspect you need to grasp as a millionaire is your capacity to conform to exchange. Change occurs all around us, and whilst you're concerned with some thing as unstable as money you need on the way to adapt to change. There are going to be days in which your money takes a chief hit, and there are going to be days wherein it will increase past your wildest goals. There are going to be days when nothing is going the manner you deliberate, and there are going to be days in which the whole thing is going perfectly. If you want to reach life you want to be organized to adapt to the modifications which can be taking area around you. There is not often something you may do to manipulate those changes, and it isn't always well worth it to strive. Instead, you need to understand that these modifications are beyond your manage and adapt the excellent manner that you could. Seek out wherein benefits can be received and use these to help develop you toward your achievement. If all else fails, exercise your potential to just accept defeat and mistakes.

Becoming a millionaire means learning the millionaire mind-set. Millionaires do no longer attain this fame with the aid of residing with restricting beliefs, poor behavior, and terrible mind-set and behaviors that don't serve their highest precise. If you want to be a millionaire you want to apprehend the fee of your mindset behaviors and how they have an effect on your lengthy-time period achievement. There is not any different way to end up a millionaire than to master yourself. The "mystery" of being a millionaire is that wealth is obtained as an instantaneous reflection of the quantity of personal success you create for your existence. The extra you practice personal development, the greater your wealth will develop.

Chapter 2: Habits Of Millionaires And Billionaires

"The chance of making monetary freedom relies upon at the device you are the usage of."

- Mark Victor Hanson

Believe it or no longer, many millionaires have behavior that you would not expect. As a mean center-earnings individual, you probable have been taught to consider that millionaires are all about having the maximum expensive wardrobe, clothes, homes, and vacations. You probably have been result in consider that they spend thousands and thousands on luxurious matters and that cash simply slips thru their fingers like water via the tap. The reality is, the opposite is proper.

Millionaires do not turn out to be millionaires through spending like millionaires. Instead, they emerge as millionaires by using recognizing the price of money and respecting it in a manner that allows them to hold it and manipulate it correctly. Most millionaires boast approximately their potential to spend as little as feasible. While they'll be shopping for homes, vehicles, and other luxuries, you may nearly definitely guarantee that they're shopping for each good buy viable alongside the way.

A millionaire gets to be a millionaire because they learn how to store cash. They study the fee of money and they learn how to spend it in a way that maintains its fee for them. The gadgets they invest in are always high high-quality and almost usually preserve their value even long after being purchased. If you want to be a millionaire, you need to learn to admire money in this same manner. The following are five millionaire conduct that you need to begin working towards at once.

Stay Positive

A high-quality attitude is worthwhile to a millionaire. If you want to be a millionaire, you want to learn to have a nice mind-set and stay that manner as often as possible. Being advantageous doesn't suggest that you don't experience bad emotions. It actually method which you know how to take those bad feelings and manipulate them successfully, and then turn the whole thing around in order that it's miles wonderful once again. If you need to be a millionaire, you have to learn to look for the silver lining in each situation.

Hang Out with Other Successful People

Millionaires dangle out with other millionaires. Those who don't earn the identical quantity as they do in reality don't have the equal mindset and therefore it's far difficult for them to be round. If a millionaire had been to spend a significant amount of time with non-millionaires, it is nearly positive that they could lose their wealth. You should always are looking for to surround yourself with different a success individuals who are heading in the same route as you are. Spending time with people who aren't will lead you backwards and could result in you now not earning as a whole lot as you doubtlessly ought to in case you spent it slow greater wisely with a better desire of people.

Pursue Your Own Goals

People who are successful don't get there by way of making an investment their complete existence in achieving different human beings's goals for them. They are not personnel, they're employers. They need to be at the top due to the fact they recognise this is where the actual income lies, and they may do anything to be there. If you're going to be a millionaire you need to learn to discover your own goals and then pursue them. Never permit all and sundry or some thing stand in your way, surely pursue them fearlessly and fiercely so that you can gain achievement on your own existence in a way that serves you.

Have A Mentor

Having a mentor is beneficial when you are in search of to become a success. They provide you with the opportunity to hop into the short lane as they are able to provide you with advice and information to help draw you forward on your commercial enterprise and in life. Having a a success mentor will assist you via influencing your existence in a superb way. By often checking in together with your mentor and operating together with them, you will always have motivation to transport forward and gain success in your existence and commercial enterprise. This will help assure which you earn hundreds of thousands.

Respect Money

Not one single millionaire disrespects cash. The only ones who do are the ones who come into big quantities unexpectedly after which hastily lose all of it due to having no respect for cash. If you are going to be a millionaire and live that manner, you need to study the fee of money and admire it in a manner in order to allow you to maintain and manipulate your money correctly. You need to apprehend the value of a dollar and continually respect that price.

Be Willing to Make Sacrifices

People who emerge as wealthy need to learn how to make sacrifices. There are many stuff you need to sacrifice in existence on the way to come to be rich. In reality, that is one of the primary reasons why people be given as real with wealth is the basis of all evil. An untrained millionaire or billionaire will give up all the maximum important matters in existence to turn out to be wealthy. While they may absolutely be capable of generate their wealth, they may in no way be able to revel in it, or their life. If you need to be a a success millionaire, you have to check what to sacrifice and while. For example, sacrifice birthday celebration time and enjoyment time to paintings, now not your family time, despite the fact that. Your own family, the people who love you, and the people you love are essential. If you want to unfastened up extra time so that you can generate your wealth, loose it up by using way of sacrificing the time you spend doing more such things as partying, searching TV, and thrilling.

You need to also be willing to sacrifice your authentic dream. As you evolve, the dream you have were given is going to alternate and therefore what you're running inside the path of may additionally even evolve. You need to be inclined to actually be for the reason that and adjust your vision and your dreams whilst you figure inside the direction of achievement for your life.

Be an Entrepreneur

You will quickly study the variations among varieties of profits, but for now you need to understand the primary method of acquiring income that you need to recognize. Linear earnings, or earnings you get right away for the paintings you do, ought to in no way be received thru a government venture, nor thru being someone else's employee. Regardless of what degree of financial protection which could provide you with, it's going to moreover offer you with monetary chains. You will in no manner be on top of factors; consequently, you can in no manner be able to inflate the income you earn through your linear deliver. You have to be willing to be an entrepreneur in case you are going to generate enough income to grow to be a millionaire or billionaire. Without being your very very own boss, you'll located a ceiling for your achievement and you could in no manner surpass what your organization is inclined to allow you to grow to.

No Excuses

Millionaires and billionaires in no way make excuses. Whether they are tired, bored, sad with the task accessible, would as an alternative be having amusing, or some issue else, they will in no way make an excuse. They understand that paintings ought to be finished, and they may be inclined to do it that lets in you to earn an profits. Without their willingness to paintings without a excuses, they will in no way earn enough of an profits to come to be a millionaire, masses less a billionaire. Putting matters off, procrastinating, and using excuses in preference to earning consequences are all conduct of those who will in no way generate wealth in their life.

Get Quality Sleep

You ought to be able to have the power to work every day, so getting excellent sleep is critical. Not every millionaire or billionaire sleeps for a complete eight hours each night time, but every one definitely makes exquisite that she or he is getting top notch sleep every time they rest their eyes. Without high-quality sleep, you could in no way have the electricity you want to hold happening a each day basis. Millionaires regularly have full schedules, and that they have to be capable of keep those schedules if they're going to hold their wealth. If you can not determine to this all due to a lack of strength then you may lose your wealth, if you even gain it within the first place. You need to constantly determine to a nice relaxation every unmarried night time.

Write Down 10 Ideas Every Day

The ideas you've got got on a normal foundation are essential. Creativity serves your entrepreneurship and therefore you want to continuously inspire yourself to live innovative. It may be pretty beneficial to get into the dependancy of writing down 10 mind every unmarried day. While no longer all of these thoughts may be useable or useful, they will maintain you operating towards generating new thoughts. Every so frequently, you will come upon an idea you give you that may be a few exclusive million-dollar-concept. When you do, positioned it into movement and bypass earn your million!

Learn to Say No

Just because opportunities gift themselves doesn't recommend you've got got got to mention positive. Being a slave to the word "yes" can keep you lousy. You need to discover ways to time desk yourself with the resource of using recognizing what sports activities are useful and worthwhile and which of them aren't. If you stretch your self too thin, you may end up spending your energy on matters that aren't useful and your financial wealth will go through as a end end result. Additionally, if some aspect does no longer serve you or make you glad, you have to not pursue it. It is truely okay to mention no to matters that are not useful on your ordinary scenario. These matters are usually, in reality, the possibility of useful and can drain your precious strength and go away you feeling sad and annoyed in the course of precious time that need to be spent focusing on how you can growth your wealth. Learn to say no.

Plant Seeds Everywhere

True people of wealth understand that there are opportunities everywhere. As a end result, they may be continuously planting seeds which will take gain of possibilities and boom their possibility of manufacturing wealth in various areas. You need to normally make an effort to plant seeds anywhere you. When you're networking, while you are confronted with favorable business corporation opportunities, if you have new mind, and each time some difficulty else comes up which could benefit your wealth in a single manner or a few distinctive, constantly plant a seed. This doesn't constantly imply that you may see to it that each seed will flourish, however it offers you the opportunity to get on board with almost a few factor that indicates complete promise, in place of being overlooked of the loop due to the fact you didn't make an effort to plant seeds.

Stand Next to The Smartest Person in The Room

There are many advantages that could come from repute next to the exceptional individual in the room. When you do, you're visible as a smart man or woman as properly, and you right away benefit some stage of social recognition in truth thru the usage of your placement in the room. As nicely, you gain the possibility to speak to them and ask questions so you can examine more about what they may be knowledgeable in. Finally, it additionally gives you the opportunity to community and get your self "in" with smarter human beings. Smarter people are generally wealthier people, so at the same time as you're "in" with these humans, you advantage the potential to increase your very personal reputation and wealth exponentially certainly primarily based mostly on those connections by myself.

Maintain Your Health

No one ever had been given rich through lying in a sanatorium mattress due to the reality they did not preserve their fitness. If you need to be rich, you have to maintain your fitness. The extra healthy you are, the greater you'll be able to live for your ft and hold pursuing your wealth and riches. You want to discover how you could maintain your fitness in a way that stops you from getting sick and serves you thru providing you with extra strength. Always consume well, and foster a workout plan a terrific way to will let you stay bodily active. The more you preserve your fitness, the extra wealth you will be able to generate for yourself.

Do The Stuff You Love Each Day

Wealthy human beings understand the price of lifestyles and that now not every minute of the day want to be spent doing art work-associated responsibilities. In truth, rich humans like to have a laugh. You must make time each unmarried day to do at the least one hassle which you really love doing. Furthermore, strive doing belongings you loved doing as a child as those are normally the purest passions which you deliver. Paint, revel in a bike, hike, observe comedian books, do something that makes your coronary coronary heart glad. This will all contribute to the super of your life, it truly is critical while you need to generate wealth.

Follow Up with People

Whether it's for business enterprise or in non-public life, you have to typically study up with humans. Follow up with customers to permit them to recognise you've been considering them and to look if they are playing their purchases, take a look at up with personnel to look if they may be pleased with their jobs, and study up with corporations and different corporations you figure with to peer how they may be feeling approximately your business employer interactions. As well, comply with up with buddies, circle of relatives, and anyone else of significance to peer how they may be doing in life. The greater you follow up with people, the higher. Personal connections are crucial at the same time as you're constructing an empire, as no empire became ever constructed on my own. You want to continuously make investments time in nurturing your connections with human beings each outside and inside of your commercial enterprise.

Be Bold

While you don't want to reinvent the wheel, you could in reality advantage from spinning it in a completely specific manner. In industrial company and in life, you need to learn how to be bold and be courageous. Take the movements that no character else is taking, make formidable actions that include risks, and flow yourself and your corporation in the direction of primary fulfillment with the aid of the use of way of ditching the "shy guy" act. It is never beneficial to be shy or timid in a placing where you want to generate achievement. Always be willing to be formidable and be brave. Talk to the individuals who appear "out of your league", take crucial steps toward change, and lift your self up closer to being notable.

Never Be in A Rush

If you find that you are rushing, you are not managing your self and some time table effectively. You must never be in a hurry. Being in a hurry leaves lose ends and it results in sloppiness. If you need to be a millionaire or a billionaire, you should learn how to manage your self and your agenda as it ought to be and never be in a hurry. Always time table masses of time for each venture to be finished.

Millionaires and billionaires who are in a hurry are continuously liable to dropping the whole thing, this is why they may be dashing. They moreover end up deteriorating their health and so their economic wealth suffers regardless. Don't permit that be you.

Learn to Communicate

Millionaires recognize the way to speak, and they are able to talk effectively. They comprehend a manner to concentrate, they realise at the same time as to speak, and that they recognize what to mention. They are normally one step in advance of the rest of the communique, so they're awesome at guiding it in any path they preference. Wealthy human beings are specially clever, and that they recognize exactly a way to use verbal exchange as certainly one of their most effective system. Since conversation is one of the number one strategies of acquiring wealthy through getting what you want and what you want, you need to discover techniques to speak effectively and effectively with the ones spherical you. Start small, and artwork your way up. Eventually, you may be able to speak with every body you preference to gain any very last outcomes you preference.

If you need to be a millionaire or a billionaire, you need to learn how to foster the conduct of 1. The greater you discover ways to tackle those conduct and observe them into your very own lifestyles, the extra success you'll generate in the direction of your dreams. Being capable of act like a millionaire now, in advance than you without a doubt have wealth, will provide you with the first-rate possibility to end up a millionaire inside the close to future. Start appearing as despite the truth that you have got were given coins within the economic organisation now, and you will see that right away the cash in fact can be for your economic group account. It isn't always the law of appeal; it is the regulation of existence.

You Must Be Better Than Everyone

"Conquer your worrying situations with the useful resource of accepting the fact which you need to be more than any project (or character) that comes your way."

-      Alex Becker

Only 1% of the populace is rich, and so as so one may be part of that 1% you want to be higher than actually every body else. There isn't always any room to be excellent and there may be no room to be first-rate, you need to be exceptional, duration. If you need to be wealthy, you want to discover ways to be higher than each unmarried different individual inside the room, or you won't be rich and it's that easy.

If you have got been to fill a room with one hundred humans and test them 40 years down the road, best 1 of those one hundred people might be wealthy. The opportunities of turning into wealthy are considerably slim, and the most effective possible possibility that allows you to end up wealthy is to accept now not some thing an awful lot much less. You want to recognize that the millionaire mind-set leaves no wiggle room to be something an lousy lot less than honestly impeccable. You have to be truly the notable at the entirety you do by using using way of being higher than anybody else who's doing it.

Of course, you are not going to be the superb proper off the bat. It is going to take you time to learn how to do matters, and it is going to take you time to discover ways to do them properly. But, in case you need to be a millionaire, you have to be committed to learning. You should be simply committed to the truth that you're going to be higher than sincerely every person else and you could do truely the whole thing interior' your electricity to see to it which you are. If you aren't inclined to determine to this degree, you could in no manner be triumphant as a millionaire.

People who aren't willing to be higher than anybody else do now not come to be rich. They end up a part of the middle splendor, or lower. At quality, they'll come to be part of the top-center elegance. But, I am guessing that you aren't proper proper here to learn how to be any diploma of center-magnificence. Instead, you need to investigate the way you will be part of the elite top-elegance society that is filled simplest with folks that are superb enough to earn themselves the wealth they choice.

Being better than absolutely everyone else may be uncomfortable. You are going to run into conditions in which you may need to be willing to confess which you are higher than others. You may additionally additionally lose friends and cherished ones due to the fact they honestly can't cope with admitting which you have finished higher than they have. You might probable emerge as surrounded by way of using manner of those who are all striving to be higher than the rest and consequently you are not always the exceptional inside the room. The component is that you're going to be uncomfortable. You want to generally be willing to paintings to be better than every person else inside the room so you can and no longer using a hassle sail into riches. Even even as you are surrounded by using people who possess extra wealth than yourself, you want to be willing to try and be the splendid within the room. It might not occur that actual minute, however artwork to make it show up inside the very near destiny.

It might be very crucial to recognize that part of being higher than all people else in the room is being confident in that know-how. If you spend your complete time inside the room displaying off how a wonderful deal better you are, you are not going to be powerful at advancing your self to more wealth. You will rapidly close down your capability to speak, pay interest, and examine, and consequently you may never get past in that you're. You need to commonly attempt to do higher than you're in recent times, because of this you need to generally be inclined to talk effectively, pay interest, and study. Being smug will in no way lead you toward achievement, nor wealth.

People who're wealthy and who are higher than others within the room are assured on this. They do not need to rub it into the faces of others. In reality, if asked they are nearly generally greater than willing to percent and art work to help others be higher as properly. They in no way take some time to expose off how masses higher they're through using way of making others feel poorly. Those who do are regularly now not as wealthy as one could probable count on, as they're often making up for it via the use of manner of talking a huge talk whilst not having something to lower returned it up.

To be truly wealthy, you should apprehend the essential stability of being better than all and sundry else in the room and being snug with that data. You have to learn how to locate consolation within the discomfort of losing friends and own family and of being treated as though you are wonderful from all of us else. After all, you're specific whilst you are part of 1% of the whole populace.

You can't erase the reality that now not everyone can be able to relate to you due to the fact now not absolutely everyone may be experiencing what you're experiencing. Not each person will recognize what it's far want to be part of that 1%, and this is the splendor of it. If they will understand, then there might be primary% because absolutely all and sundry might be wealthy and wealth would be of little to no importance. If you want to be simply wealthy, you need to discover ways to come to phrases with this now. Only then will you be succesful of truly include the wealthy way of life and lead your self into being a millionaire. So, are you willing to confess that you are destined to be better than truly each person else that you realize?

Chapter 3: Types Of Income

"The 2nd you're making passive profits and portfolio income part of your life, your life will exchange. Those phrases will become flesh."

- Robert Kiyosaki

There are forms of income that millionaires and billionaires use to generate their wealth. These are the number one kinds which is probably responsible for their potential to create enough wealth that they might do in fact a few thing they desire. The types are: linear income and passive income.

Linear Income

Linear income is a completely number one sense of profits. It is the cash you get for the paintings you do, whether or not it is a profession call you hold or a challenge you've got accomplished for someone else. Linear profits is an critical supply of profits for really anybody, or maybe the richest people in the world hold to utilize linear income as an possibility to generate wealth. However, linear profits should not be depended on by myself. Those who rely totally on linear income will typically be a slave to their career or task, due to the reality with out it they'll no longer supply any wealth-making opportunities. In addition for your linear income, you want to feature severa forms of passive earnings.

Passive Income

Passive income is a obligatory part of generating and maintaining millionaire fame. People who want to come to be millionaires take a look at the cost of passive income and a way to comprehend it. Passive income is the sort of profits that you earn at the same time as you sleep. If you'll keep in mind the degrees of wealth, stage five consists of of the quantity of folks that generate coins at the same time as they are sound asleep.

There are infinite numbers of passive profits circulate you could acquire, but millionaires most effective interact in the ones in an effort to absolutely make an effect on their profits degrees. If you want to increase the amount of earnings you are incomes, then the following seven forms of passive income are critical that allows you to explore. These options will permit you to earn an income at the same time as you sleep, helping you with transferring toward the whole lot you need to be to be a actual millionaire.

Earning a passive profits allows you to make money effects. It will growth the remarkable of your existence by using manner of offering you with the possibility to stay virtually. You save you having to artwork so tough for your earnings and also you start being capable of paintings in techniques which can be more powerful and powerful. You supply yourself a cushion to make errors or declare defeat, which is essential when you are leading a millionaire life-style.

Method #1: Selling Evergreen Products

Evergreen products are any product which can stand on my own with out you having to do something more even as you are making the sale. Live courses or activities and programs require you to genuinely set up paintings in skip lower back for the earnings you are gaining. However, say you have been to jot down a e-book, launch a self-paced route, or sell a video with crucial statistics for effective humans. This sort of product has already been completed, so all the income you are making come from effective advertising and marketing plans. You do now not have to do any additional paintings for the income you are receiving, you are honestly done through this element.

Evergreen merchandise are a effective way to promote and earn earnings on the same time as you are sleeping. By taking your statistics you can prepare a stand-by myself product, have a touchdown net web page made to your income, marketplace the product and sell it. You can both do all the paintings of advertising and advertising, or you may outsource this aspect and hiring a marketing and marketing manager to cowl this part of your business corporation. Then, you sincerely earn all of the income from the profits.

Method #2: Real Estate Investments

Real belongings investments are an desire for human beings who've a higher profits, and that they've a excessive amount of capacity. When you get into real assets, there are numerous tactics that you can earn money and growth your profits. Rental homes, holiday leases, and flipping houses are all top notch possibilities to put money into actual belongings and make cash decrease back.

If you want to assemble your income via rental homes and excursion rentals, you may need to get a few cash in the back of you so you can without a doubt purchase those residences. Once you have got got, you could get renters into each property and begin profiting! Rental homes are an incredible lengthy-time period funding because you benefit a small quantity of profits up the front, as soon as the property is paid off you get substantially greater every month from apartment costs, and every time making a decision to you could sell the assets and earn a huge profits from it.

Flipping houses is any other awesome way to make coins from actual property. You can invest in foreclosed homes or cheaper fixer-uppers and then restore the region up and flip it. There are many pointers, mind, and regulations spherical flipping houses on the manner to make it a a success supply of income for you. If you pick out out to get into flipping houses you have to take some time to analyze this selection and the way it genuinely works to make sure which you maximize your income from this challenge.

Nearly all of us who has a huge amount of cash is invested in real belongings in a single way or each other. Real property is a few element with a purpose to constantly be profitable as human beings are generally going to want homes. If you need to spend money on real belongings, you'll almost honestly get your coins lower once more plus greater each single time.

Method #3: Outsource Work

One manner to show earned profits into passive profits is to outsource the work you are doing. For example, if you are constructing a commercial enterprise business enterprise you may start outsourcing severa elements of your art work, ultimately outsourcing the whole lot so that you can popularity your interest some other place on earning earnings via a contemporary or opportunity technique.

Outsourcing can be completed in masses of techniques, you could rent new earnings personnel, assistants, advertising groups, and definitely each different wide shape of employees to run your business company. The extra personnel you rent, the greater passive your earnings will become. It is vital that you continuously make sure which you are hiring the right people for your institution, but, as hiring the wrong ones can result in you losing earnings. It is not beneficial to have a person in a feature if they may be now not capable of generating the consequences you're seeking out.

Method #4: Investment Portfolios

Having a wealthy funding portfolio can paintings on your determine on when it comes to growing your profits. There are many unique strategies that you may make investments, from making an funding in shares, to developing an investment in mutual rate variety and one in all a kind techniques. You can invest in your non-public together at the side of your very very own expertise, however ideally you have to work together with an funding company that will help you. Financial advisors and funding entrepreneurs are mainly skilled with turning investments into extra earnings, so that they will let you make the proper options to make sure that you earn most make the maximum of your investments.

One element you need to take a look at is that a rich investment portfolio is one that is rather various. You want a good way to recognize this and put money into as many precise extraordinary areas as possible. The greater you make investments, the much more likely you are going so as to growth the quantity of earnings you're making. It additionally lets in mitigate hazard and prevent you from losing big quantities of coins.

Method #five: Royalty Income

Earning royalty income is an exquisite possibility to earn a passive earnings. Royalties are received via taking detail in someone else's mission after which incomes royalties due to your involvement. Aside out of your involvement in developing the undertaking, you do now not must perform a little element with reference to keeping it, advertising and marketing it, or otherwise building the challenge. All you need to do is uphold your part of the deal after which the rest falls into area.

If you play your playing cards proper, royalties will pay you a massive amount of money. You can earn cash on an ongoing foundation for a long term duration so long as you make investments a while into tasks which can be superb to be a achievement. Always make certain to look at as a extraordinary deal as you can approximately the challenge in advance, after which assuming it is a superb funding of it slow, go in advance and make investments. That will lead you to correctly receiving royalty earnings on art work you have got completed.

Method #6: Startup Investments

Once you have got sufficient cash to make investments, it is a fantastic idea to maintain in mind making an investment in startup groups. The commonplace silent investor or angel investor need to be capable of invest at the least $a hundred,000 into startups a good way to be concerned, but as quickly as you could acquire this factor it is a brilliant possibility to growth your internet properly nicely worth all at once.

Before you begin investing in startup agencies you want to take the time to research what goes into creating a a fulfillment startup. Take a while to study from different customers and recognize how you may invest your cash in a way that mitigates your danger and ensures that you have the very best risk of gaining your coins again. When you do this, you make certain which you are informed enough to show those investments into a valuable earnings movement. If you do now not need to begin making an investment in startups in your very very own, you can keep in thoughts getting in with a companion or a small institution of traders within the beginning. Doing this may help you study the ropes and may hold you from risking too much of your coins into startups in advance than you are absolutely informed inside the manner to make investments in the proper ones.

Method #7: Franchising

Another brilliant manner to earn passive profits is to franchise your commercial enterprise organisation. If you have got a sort of business agency that may be franchised, franchising it could earn you a large passive profits. With franchises, you can earn money from each new chain that is unfold out. As a end end result, you could earn cash from distinctive humans starting their private groups below you.

Franchising can be a bit tough earlier than the entirety and it can take some thoughtful planning to get started out out, but as soon as your business company is up and taking walks you could start earning main advantage from this corporation version. If you do no longer presently have a business organization that can be franchised, you need to hold in thoughts starting off a organization that could later be franchised. Work on building up the initial industrial organisation and as soon because it's massive sufficient you could invest within the method of turning it right into a franchise. Then you can benefit in all the benefits of being the primary owner of a franchise chain.

Passive income offers you with a powerful opportunity to revel in real economic protection. This isn't always the sort of financial protection that consists of you having a guaranteed paycheck at the give up of each pay duration from your organisation. Instead, it way that you are actually getting cash while you sleep and that you are incomes even greater at the equal time as you in reality strive. When you are able to earn passive earnings in this way, you open your self as much as revel in real financial freedom. You can begin doing some thing you preference because of the truth you understand that you could have a regular stream of income coming your way irrespective of what you're doing. Of course, in case you need to be a millionaire and stay one, you will be spending a while invested inside the subsequent maximum essential commercial enterprise organisation project you'll be pursuing. Remember, stage five wealth consists of you being worthwhile at the same time as you sleep, and passive earnings is the crucial element so you can try this.

Chapter 4: Take Advantage Of The Internet

The internet has produced more millionaires nowadays than almost some other enterprise platform. It is not any mystery that in this point in time, the internet is a treasured beneficial resource which will can help you accomplish simply a few element you purchased all the way right down to achieve. If you want to be a millionaire, you want to embody the net, take gain of it, and learn how to leverage it as an income-producing possibility.

There are many methods to use the internet on your gain. It starts offevolved with expertise the manner the net may be used and figuring out techniques that you may personally use it to generate earnings. Following that, you could start constructing up your basis and launching your new profits-generating approach. You should use the net to set up at least taken into consideration one in each of your earnings resources. The following are five thoughts of methods you can begin incomes an profits online and turning it into both a passive or linear earnings flow into.

YouTube Star

YouTube is popping out stars left, right and center and there may be no longer a few factor to mention you could't be one in every of them! YouTube has the capability to assist earn you numerous hundreds of bucks via filming, which you may do from any immoderate remarkable video virtual digicam. There are YouTube channels approximately truely any situation remember range you can consider. You can locate channels with entertainers who provide comedy for visitors, you can locate business enterprise agency-oriented channels who educate you about advertising and marketing and advertising and marketing and running a employer, you can find channels that educate you approximately severa interests and competencies. There are limitless subjects for what YouTube channels can feature.

If you need to take gain of YouTube and begin incomes an income thru filming your self, you can get started out out extremely clean. All you need is a excessive first-rate digital digicam and a modern creativeness. Think about some factor you're obsessed on similarly to knowledgeable in and start filming approximately it! You can educate, entertain, or maybe without a doubt share. There are many vloggers to be had who percentage daily statistics about their lives and make cash doing it! All you need is the choice to make money and the potential to apply a virtual digital camera and add your movies to YouTube. From there, you monetize your motion pix, carry out a piece fundamental advertising and viola you've got got a a achievement YouTube channel!

There are many YouTube stars who're earning enough to buy homes, motors, and a few component else they preference. They are in a function to show their YouTube channel into their complete-time earnings and as a cease end result they could do something they need, as long as they may be filming on a regular basis. If you need to take benefit of on line income resources, YouTube is a super vicinity to begin.

Online Retailer

If you aren't as digicam savvy, you can endure in thoughts an opportunity such as starting up an internet retail hold. Online shops make masses of greenbacks each year, and the quantity of growth you may hold is limitless. The outstanding earnings-producing on-line retail model is to start a dropshipping employer. This manner, you do no longer need to pay a huge sum of money to achieve inventory and deliver it to your clients. Instead, all inventory and delivery-related responsibilities are controlled via your wholesaler. All you want to do is run the internet site, plug in products, and marketplace your internet page! You may additionally additionally even outsource the internet site protection and advertising and marketing positions to distinctive individuals who need to supply an earnings online just so your online store profits is actually passive.

Online stores have many blessings to being capable of plug into the marketplace. You have a worldwide market right off the bat, which means that you can intention any section of the market and reach a notably higher quantity of your goal marketplace than you may if you had a bodily store the front which you had been attempting to find to promote. The overhead and startup expenses are a fraction of what it prices to start a brick and mortar commercial enterprise, and you could do almost some thing you choice along with your industrial company. Simply examine Amazon.Com: they started out out as an internet ebook keep and feature considering the truth that advanced into selling definitely everything you could keep in mind. They are genuinely an internet market for diverse stores and due to their creative platform they were able to create a multi-billion-dollar corporation this is primary the net retail business enterprise.

Blogger

Believe it or now not, bloggers are nonetheless relevant in the online area and now have the potential to make a huge amount of cash on-line. Many people count on that walking a weblog is on its manner out, however there are various blogs which might be doing better than ever. The fact is that blogs make up a large a part of the net area. Many humans depend on blogs for studies features, specifically in visiting, manner of lifestyles, and consumerism situations. When human beings are trying to take a enjoy or buy a brand new item, as an example, they will frequently talk over with their preferred on-line blogs to discover which of them are the superb investments. Likewise, if someone is on the lookout for to enhance their house, purchase a brand new material cupboard, or otherwise make a sizeable exchange in their manner of lifestyles, they'll frequently are attempting to find recommendation from a weblog to see wherein the cutting-edge inclinations are heading that lets in you to live current.

Blogging is pretty clean and it doesn't take a lot to begin. Simply use a platform like WordPress or Blogger and begin typing away! With some advertising and marketing and monetization, you will be in a role to show your weblog into an profits-incomes resource proper away. It is a awesome way to earn a blog on the equal time as tapping into your market and developing the amount of fee you want to offer modern clients. Blogging is frequently considered to be an remarkable addition to any on line or offline commercial enterprise employer.

Affiliate Marketing

If you need to take subjects a step in addition, you need to hold in mind accomplice advertising. This isn't continually community advertising, irrespective of the fact that community advertising can earn you a huge amount as properly, however companion advertising and marketing and advertising is the device wherein you determine together with organizations to promote their merchandise. In go lower back, they pay you a rate off of every sale you are making for them.

Turning associate marketing and marketing and advertising into an income-generating hobby is straightforward. As lengthy as you've got an internet presence, you could end up a a fulfillment partner marketer. The more on-line presences you have got were given had been given on diverse systems, the extra profits you are going a great manner to produce via accomplice advertising and marketing and advertising. You can promote your companion hyperlinks on YouTube, blogs, social media systems, or maybe inside the offline region even as you are talking to buddies and circle of relatives. There are many groups that offer affiliate programs, along with smaller indie corporations and larger ones like Amazon.Com. You can take gain of these structures to help enhance your earnings in famous, or use it as a sidekick toward some other online-earnings-producing pastime so you can boom the quantity of earnings you are generating inside the on-line region.

Design an App

There is an app for nearly everything nowadays, and for a fantastic cause. Apps are a remarkable tool to use on clever telephones, pc systems, capsules, and awesome cellular gadgets that humans are continuously plugged into. They provide consolation, sources, amusement, and different treasured property to human beings's mobile devices. Using apps should make your mobile device a extra customized version of what you need and need at the equal time as you're carrying it round with you.

Designing an app and promoting it is able to provide you with the opportunity to earn passive profits on-line. If you produce a immoderate extraordinary app and promote it you could earn between $zero.Ninety nine and $14.Ninety 9 in keeping with download, with the not unusual resting among $1.Ninety 9 and $4.Ninety 9. With a right advertising and advertising method in area you can earn as an awful lot or as little as you want thru selling your app, all based on how an entire lot attempt you are setting into the advertising technique. A remarkable trouble about apps is that you may definitely replace your app and sell all of all of it all yet again as a more recent, updated version of the app that humans have grown to recognize and love. This keeps your market clean and maintains the lifespan of your app to be one that is longer than every different product that can truely be promoted after which die out as soon as the preliminary model has been ate up by using the aim market.

There are many one of a kind methods to take gain of the internet to supply earnings, however the ones are definitely the most handy ones to the commonplace man or woman. If you want to end up a millionaire, it's miles essential that you don't forget about approximately the price of on line enterprise. Tapping into this rich resource can provide you with the possibility to earn a significantly higher amount of earnings via little to no strive. A super factor about online corporations is that you can lease digital assistants and the agency may be actually run for you, making the profits go with the flow distinctly passive. There are many opportunities to experience the internet region, even if you are not rather professional with the net and pc structures. It severely can pay to take advantage of the profits possibilities which might be made to be had by means of the internet.

Chapter 5: The Power Of Your Team

"Ultimately, management is not about super crowning acts. It's about keeping your group targeted on a intention and induced to do their first rate to gain it, in particular even as the stakes are immoderate and the consequences certainly depend. It is set laying the muse for others' success, and then recognition decrease lower lower back and letting them shine."

-       Chris Hadfield

No one have end up a millionaire through themselves, not even a lottery winner. Lottery winners win because every body who performs has religion that someone will win and therefore they all throw in a few bucks and in the long run a person wins it. Self-made millionaires get there due to the fact they understand the price in their organization and they invest in their organization, therefore their institution invests in them and they come to be millionaires.

If you need to be a millionaire, you need to understand the power of your institution. You want to always work inside the direction of making your institution extra powerful, and every preference you are making need to be for the advantage of your group.

Pick an Experienced Team

Before you start selecting who your crew individuals are going to be, you need to recognize the importance of having an professional group. Just because of the fact you aren't completely skilled in every state of affairs doesn't suggest that your group shouldn't be. Establishing a alternatively professional crew can give you the gain of getting expertise on your facet. Just due to the fact you don't continually understand what you're doing doesn't suggest no man or woman else need to. A group that has been via the enjoy in advance than and is aware about the way to create fulfillment can draw you ahead into fulfillment an entire lot extra swiftly than you may through yourself, or with a set who changed into beneath licensed.

When you are building your business enterprise, do not forget each issue of your commercial commercial enterprise business enterprise and life and construct your group hence. Pick parents which may be going to be a primary asset to your organization and life. If you are paying them a earnings, commonly invest within the maximum expert employee you could have sufficient cash. More regularly than now not, this funding will pay off big time in the long run when they help launch you in advance into crucial achievement.

Think of your crew as your empire. You can not create an empire by using yourself, and you can't create a great empire with a network of beneath licensed folks that do now not care to paintings collectively towards a common goal. It is critical that you paintings in the direction of the commonplace purpose as an professional unit, with all and sundry being talented in their respective place of business organization. This manner, you can all depend on every exceptional to efficaciously complete his or her a part of the system and you may count on that success will come as a result.

Creating the Perfect Team

Picking your group can be a frightening mission, but it's also the most vital one. Before you hire all of us or choose all people to play to your group, you want to recognize the 5 number one factors of choosing humans on your crew. Being able to apprehend those and use them to your advantage will make sure that you are building a hard and fast this is licensed and so one can deliver you ahead into achievement.

Always Identify Weak Spots

Before you begin hiring certainly all of us to be part of your institution, understand your inclined spots. You have to furthermore pick out out your strengths. Ideally, you want to hire humans whose strengths are your weaknesses. That manner, you each have a unique responsibility to meet so that you can deliver you beforehand for your business company.

Another manner you need to recognize weaknesses is to apprehend the strengths and weaknesses in extraordinary people. In doing so, you may be capable of rent extra organization individuals so as to complement the triumphing institution you've got already created. You want to make sure that the whole organization is created mindfully so as that all of them paintings collectively in a way so that you can make certain your success. If you've got were given folks that struggle or who do now not work collectively properly, you may grow to be compromising your achievement.

Identify Your Time Commitments

In the start, you could want to be modest approximately how many humans you are hiring. Consider what it sluggish commitments are, and apprehend how an lousy lot time you need every characteristic to decide to their system. It is critical to apprehend how regularly you'll need certain jobs completed in order to your whole team to paintings productively. Once you understand this, you can rent element- and complete-time employees to fill each respective role. It is likewise crucial, however, that you apprehend the price of an superb employee. If you discover a person who is in fact certified however can simplest paintings detail-time in location of entire-time, you could recall hiring them and hiring an additional component-time worker to make up for the last time. Valuable personnel who can end up a high asset for your institution must in no manner be not noted except you certainly need to.

Discover Potential Candidates

Take some time to genuinely apprehend who your functionality candidates are. Right off the bat, you will probable recognize that some people are sick in shape for the machine. However, as soon as it entails choosing the precise man or woman, you want to sincerely emerge as important over who you are deciding on. The final choice should be a person who compliments your institution, works well collectively along with your present frame of human beings, and may help draw you ahead to your business enterprise organization. They need to be a real asset to your group.

Take the time to look through all people's software application, go through in mind their interview, and weigh their strengths and weaknesses. Are they going to be reliable and capable of captivating the place you're looking for to fill? Will they've the capacity that will help you in vital additives of industrial company, or are they going to fall flat and go away you setting? It is crucial that you select parents that are dependable and who might be committed for your achievement, recognizing that your fulfillment will also identical achievement for themselves.

Have Conversations

If you apprehend a person who might likely healthy perfectly on your institution, it is not normally crucial in case you need to have a proper interview. Instead, take a seat them down and feature a verbal exchange with them. Let them recognize approximately your commercial commercial enterprise business enterprise and your possibility and increase a formal offer to them. This will provide them the possibility to discover approximately what you're doing and come to be part of your employer within the event that they preference.

Always ensure that you maintain this verbal exchange formal enough to be about business, but no longer too formal. When you're working with human beings you understand, they usually received't want to be handled like you are a whole boss over them. Understand the charge they may be capable of upload and commonly live personable with them. If you aren't cautious, you may become pulling a strength enjoy and losing an outstanding pal, as well as the involvement of a treasured worker.

Hire The Right People and Pay Them Well

If you need to have the absolute great group, you want to be inclined to rent the pleasant humans. The first-rate human beings to your institution are the ones which is probably well at what you aren't. If you are awesome at speaking however are not brilliant at discovering, you need to rent an splendid researcher. If you are extremely good at executing plans however horrible at developing them, you want to hire an extraordinary planner. When you hire folks that excel at your weaknesses, you construct an indestructible group that allows you to guide you towards absolute greatness.

In addition to hiring the terrific humans, you want to pay them the extremely good wages. If you do now not deal with your private, they'll not deal with you in skip again. Instead, they may ultimately head off within the route of someone else who's willing to deal with them higher. When you get the right people to your institution, you should do the whole thing inside' your strength to hold them for your group. This includes paying them what they ought to be paid, that is an exquisite revenue to healthy their awesome competencies.

Constantly Assess Your Team

Just because of the reality your team has been constructed doesn't mean that you are accomplished. You have to constantly be assessing your business enterprise for opportunities to reinforce it. You continuously want to apprehend where your strengths and weaknesses are, as this is what will come up with the records you want to be successful. Knowing in which your weaknesses are offers you the capacity to hire new frame of people or make required changes to make certain that those weaknesses are being offset by way of proficient workforce.

You need to have a system in region in which you look into your staff on a normal foundation. Take the time to bear in mind in which they'll be at and what kind of asset they're imparting your business enterprise with. If they're now not proving to be an asset for your group, discover a way to give them the opportunity to boom their productivity, or maintain in thoughts letting them flow in select of a person else who will do a higher task.

Your organization, whether or not it's miles in corporation or in lifestyles, is a critical a part of you being able to succeed. If you want to obtain existence and in employer, you need so that you may want to have a group behind you who's privy to the way to work collectively with a view to produce achievement. You need to be capable of receive as actual with that your crew is going to art work inside the course of not unusual desires and assist bring you ahead at every chance they get. If you do no longer have a sturdy team in location, or in case you don't have a group the least bit, it's far crucial which you positioned one collectively. A sturdy institution will give you the belongings, charge, and knowledge which you want that allows you to turn out to be a millionaire. Not one single millionaire got there with out the assist of a collection, and you won't every.

Take The Pledge

"You're the cause pressure of your non-public existence, don't permit every body thieve your seat."

- Unknown

If you have controlled to live devoted to this ebook and test until now, then it is almost notable which you are prepared to turn out to be a millionaire. Becoming a millionaire calls for paintings, perseverance, determination, recognition, and a willingness to succeed. If you accept as real with you studied you've got were given what it takes, then it is time in an effort to take the millionaire pledge.

The millionaire pledge is simple, however it is severe. In order that allows you to come to be a millionaire, you need to be capable of decide to this pledge. Without it, you may no longer have the dedication that you need a good way to see your aim thru. Let this be your first lesson in effective intention making plans.

The pledge is simple for you to finish. You without a doubt take a easy piece of paper, and write down the following:

"I, (insert your name), vow that I will do some issue it takes for me to turn out to be a millionaire. I apprehend that it'll take numerous difficult paintings, strength of will, and perseverance, and I determine to devoting myself to this purpose. I will do some issue it takes to ensure that I benefit this aim effectively. I apprehend that there may be tough instances, and that there can be factors in which I must give up and take transport of my errors. I am organized to artwork inside the path of the fulfillment of my motive know-how that those inevitable activities will upward thrust up, likely often over. I decide to seeing myself thru this purpose and incomes a million bucks, and from there incomes numerous more. I will not stop till I emerge as a millionaire."

Once you've got written this down, or your very personal custom designed variant of it, sign the paper, date it, and location it someplace that you could see it on a each day basis. By bodily seeing your willpower written down on a normal basis, you'll be capable of live real to it and you will notably growth your possibilities of reaching it. Affirming your intention on a every day basis is a high-quality manner to maintain it sparkling on your thoughts and stay brought about closer to attaining it.

It is important that you make the technique of witnessing your pledge a ritual that allows you to artwork with you toward your success. Give yourself the possibility to definitely sense inspired and stimulated via the pledge, and vow that you could continuously allow it to infuse your thoughts with fantastic thoughts at the same time as you are looking at it. You need to in no way have a look at your pledge with a horrible mind-set or with the perception that you could not gather it. If you do, you need to rewrite the pledge and begin over. Never tarnish your dream with thoughts of disbelief.

Chapter 6: The Wonder Of The Worldview

Do you spot a pitcher 1/2 of-whole or half of-empty? Rather, do you note the glass the least bit? Or do you spend all of your time looking for a higher glass? Well, if you aren't cautious, that cup has the capability to swallow you complete!

Your worldviewdefines what you do, why and the way you do it, and what now not doing it'll do to you. If there can be one thing you discern on, then make it your worldview. Because as soon as that modifications, the entirety for your life shifts to fit your narrative. On the opposite, an unchanged thoughts-set will offer you with the same antique outcomes no matter how difficult you attempt within the superb areas of life.

Many people usually usually have a tendency to push aside the importance of worldview, calling it "some new-age highbrow fluff and mumbo-jumbo." But guess what? This is a studies-sponsored technological information. In psychology, researchers talk about a few factor referred to as self-appealing prophecies. I recognize what you're wondering: the time period "prophecies" in all likelihood does now not help in convincing you it's now not mumbo-jumbo. But concentrate this out.

Self-stunning prophecies are predictions you're making about yourself that finally come to be real, truely because of the fact you're taking shipping of as actual with in them strongly. There are not any mystical forces at play proper right here. Here's the way it certainly works. Have you ever gotten up within the morning and "truely acknowledged" that it's going to be a horrific day nowadays? Many human beings are quite appropriate at choosing on that inkling. And most customarily that inkling is quite spot on. The day you have got got had been for the reason that "feeling" constantly seems to be terrible. You bypass over your subway to paintings, the person that receives you your morning espresso messes up the order, you recognize your boss is having a in particular cranky day, and on is going the distress. You can't expect the day to be over. The fine problem properly well well worth appreciating about the day is your 6th revel in is getting a chunk more potent each single time! Is it despite the fact that?

Let's rewind the day to look if changing the worldview makes any difference to this "horrible day." The same day, identical you. You sit up straight to your bed and you have got a strange feeling love it is probably a terrible day. But then in preference to jumping directly to the depressing conclusions' bandwagon, you tell your self a few component to the effect of, "Okay permit's see how this appears." You get organized, attain the subway, best to have a look at it tempo proper away as you step directly to the platform. The subsequent one comes and also you discover that it has a seat for you while the preceding one modified into absolutely packed. You head straight away to the office, in which the man or woman switches up your preferred espresso for some other taste. You don't like now not having your normal coffee but furthermore comprehend that this special flavor isn't too horrible each. You may not have it every day however it's actual to shuffle your everyday once in a while. You skip on to appearance your boss who is not in a extraordinary mood. So you try to be a hint more empathetic, asking if there may be some thing you can do. The boss doesn't say a excellent deal however you understand his behavior in the direction of you shifts and he is also a chunk nicer.

This is how self-gratifying prophecies art work. If you accept as true with a few component can't be accomplished, you give up on it subconsciously and due to the reality you give up, your efforts aren't what they might be in any other case, therefore the failure. What's greater is you're taking this failure as a affirmation of your belief and the cycle goes on. The amazing manner to interrupt the cycle is to change the attitude most effective a tad.

Beliefs That Are Holding You Back

Now that we've seen the lifestyles-changing distinction an altered mind-set can supply, it's time to have a look at the ideals that make up this worldview. The definition of the time period belief is pretty exciting. A perception is something this is taken to be proper regardless of the fact that there may not be precise proof to useful useful resource it.

The human thoughts is usually yearning for meaning. So it makes use of those beliefs to make feel of the endless data that is continuously pouring in. Without the ones subjects to arrange this statistics, human belief would possibly possibly fall apart like a house of cards. There is actually one problem in this scheme of factors—ideals are an precis, unscientific entity. We take the ones on from our households, cultures, and societies at huge. Once usual, we lodge to these identical classes to make revel in of the latest data too, even if the latest facts won't be absolutely nicely proper with the triumphing ideals.

An instance regularly stated on this regard is that of informed elephants. The taking walks footwear don't teach grown elephants. That might also possibly be impossible. Think about it—why may a large animal like that pay attention to a person who may be beaten if the elephant makes a choice? This mature elephant can be very aware of its electricity. On the opportunity hand, a little one elephant has no idea of its energy or functionality. All that the trainer has to do is chain it up for the first few years, simply prolonged sufficient for it to don't forget that the person is in fee.

You'd suppose that because the elephant grows, it would probably need more potent restraints. But the truth is exactly the opposite. As it grows, it learns that it's helpless. It starts offevolved believing that there's not anything more to be executed. Now, the teacher can tie up the huge animal with a flimsy rope and the elephant will in spite of the reality that consider that he can't break out his scenario.

The identical principle is at art work with human beings. Isn't it exquisite what our minds can make us take delivery of as proper with? Most often it is those distorted perceptions that hold us again. Thomas Corley (2016) studied 233 rich human beings over the route of 5 years. He discovered that the ones rich human beings had certain steadfast ideals that their awful or maybe center-beauty counterparts lacked. The most powerful of those have been the ideals in themselves, their problem-fixing capacities, and their goals and goals. While the lousy spent maximum of their lives searching ahead to failure and doubting themselves, the wealthy focused on inculcating a thoughts-set that optimized wealth introduction to the most diploma. So, what are those beliefs and the way do you consist of them into your lifestyles? In the following sections, we communicate components that assist us domesticate an unstoppable millionaire thoughts-set.

Optimism Is Key

An positive mindset is again and again related to a hit millionaires. These are the folks that exhibit a hopeful predisposition inside the course of the future further to the humans surrounding them. Three vital factors of this high-quality thoughts-set have regularly been decided to be a simply sturdy choice to gain, an unfailing religion that matters will in the end schooling session, and in all likelihood the maximum vital is the potential to be quite unnerved thru failure.

I have heard humans saying multiple instances, "You want to be born into wealth to come to be that rich. No one gets there in reality via using manner of jogging tough." There is a fragment of fact in that assertion, in particular the second a part of that announcement. No one receives there simply through way of running hard. Indeed. But the number one thing is clearly as misunderstood as most different matters approximately money. It is essential to examine that most millionaires and billionaires aren't born wealthy. Rather, it's miles the strain to go away their poorer days inside the lower back of that pushes them inside the route of greatness. No don't forget the problems they have a sturdy urge to reach and an undying faith in a higher the following day.

But that's now not all that drives the ones millionaires. There is also the sturdy perception of their very very very own introduction as well as inside the notion that they could make a contribution to growing lifestyles higher. Therefore, it isn't absolutely the want that the future might be revitalizing but moreover the ambition and the steadfast perception that they themselves could make it so.

While the optimists are so full of wonder inside the route of existence, the pessimists are entire of doubt. You may additionally word wonder and doubt each have an unknown detail but how every method this uncertainty makes all the distinction. Millionaires recognize, however lots we can also hate it, lifestyles goes to bring in misery, sincerely as it does satisfaction. And it will inflict this ache and negativity on optimists and pessimists alike. So why now not dance while it rains as opposed to cry approximately your preferred healthful being drenched?

Research indicates that tremendous behaviors can be defined the usage of 3 critical additives. That is to say, those who persevere commonly will be inclined to behave in a way that famous a predictable pattern alongside the lines of these factors—permanence, pervasiveness, and personalization.

Permanence refers back to the notion about the length of the impeding elements. The extraordinary millionaires, for instance, take delivery of as authentic with that elements that cause undesirable sports of their lives are short. On the opposite, folks who give up without issues accept as true with that there will in no way be a trade in those factors and that they are consequently, extra eternal in nature. In certainly one of a type phrases, optimists would in all likelihood say some element like, "Cut him a few slack, he is probably just having a awful day," whilst a pessimist might in all likelihood have a extra foreboding evaluation like, "There is not any issue speakme to him, he by no means takes complaint properly." Similarly, at the same time as looking at first rate situations, optimists take delivery of as authentic with the reasons of suitable sports as extra eternal while pessimists take delivery of as actual with those to be pretty temporary. For instance, at the same time as a pessimist says, "Oh that end up certainly appropriate fortune!", an optimist would in all likelihood exude loads more self assurance with the aid of pronouncing, "My correct fortune usually walks with me."

Pervasiveness is likewise a bit comparable in that it is involved with how thousands one generalizes. So, on the equal time as permanence is generalization throughout time, pervasiveness is generalization during situations. For instance, pessimists could possibly ensure statements that they believe take a look at to anybody in that category like, "All bosses are blood-sucking monsters." On the opportunity hand, an optimist can also say some factor like, "My boss may be tough at instances but it doesn't propose all bosses are the same."

And sooner or later, we speak approximately personalization, the tendency to function activities to both self or others. People with excessive conceitedness blame subjects on others even as humans with low conceitedness do not forget themselves to be the wrongdoer, regardless of the scenario. The positive millionaires, however, all over again show off the ability to stroll the tightrope almost seamlessly. These are the oldsters which might be neither narcissistic nor self-blaming. They have mastered the art of taking duty for their non-public moves with out beating themselves over them.

Becoming a Realistic Optimist

What millionaires get proper is the extremely good recipe for optimism—on the equal time as and in which to be constructive, how masses optimism is proper, and furthermore while not to be super. They apprehend optimism is not a reckless implementation of positivity. They recognize that pessimism additionally has a eager survival excellent associated with it. Imagine our ancestors, plucking and eating each berry they came for the duration of because of the fact they have been fortunately constructive about the manner topics should turn out. That wouldn't have served their aim of surviving within the wild. What's crucial is finding a middle ground that helps you to get hold of and experience the arena as it's miles and however take into account that you could change it for the higher.

Optimism often has a terrible rap a number of the self-proclaimed realists.

Most humans take transport of as real with optimism and realism are come what may additionally contradictory. The advocates of optimism rally with their timeless love for positivity while the realists protest this fantastical adherence to the positivity make-don't forget. However, most of the time, neither gets the concept of optimism proper.

So how do you discover that worldview that is the best amount of optimistic, pessimistic, and sensible? The idea is to research our ABCs all all all over again. The ABC, or the adversity-perception-result model, is a favorite some of the conduct alternate strategists. Identifying the ones three elements could have a tremendous effect at the effect that matters appear to have on us.

This version has an empowering effect on most humans. People normally be given as proper with that the sports of their environment are what purpose them to experience a particular manner. For instance, A, which stands for adversity, can be that the boss shoots down one among your thoughts in a group assembly. The C, which stands for results of the A, is that you are so overpowered via way of this scary bout of self-doubt that you decide to hold your mouth near for the relaxation of the interaction. It is form of automated, isn't it? And for the reason that you may't manage what the boss does, you really need to stay with this doomed feeling. There isn't always any manner spherical it. But in keeping with this version, what you pass over is the important B, which stands for notion in among adversity and results. In this situation, the belief perhaps some component like, "The boss is proper, and it is silly. I need to NEVER do some element stupid, and actually everybody want to usually have a exquisite view of me!" Sure, this seems like an exaggeration but consider me, that is what most humans do with out even figuring out it.

Now, permit's trade this B just a little: "The boss didn't like my idea but that doesn't make it stupid. It's no longer obligatory that everybody likes my thoughts all the time." The 2d I take the stress off, I am loads tons a lot much less in all likelihood to spend the relaxation of the assembly brooding and wallowing about a few issue that have become no longer in my control within the first vicinity.

Most millionaires are very plenty privy to their ABC. It is due to this focus and steady paintings on their ideals that they may make picks that might be taken into consideration unstable or reckless but however seem to pay off most of the time. Having stated that, this recognition won't come truly to us. The conversations we've got got had been given with ourselves have grow to be so ingrained in our systems that we might not even recognise the ideals that we're breeding. That is why, in the next phase, we talk the way to address yourself-talk and restructure the distorted beliefs.

The Stories You Tell Yourself

As brilliantly extremely good as our thoughts is, it is also a tad naive. It believes all that we tell it. And now not without a doubt that but it places all efforts gathering proof to show all that we tell it. You don't want to recognise the complete psychology theories in this subject depend to apprehend that a little one who has been supported and encouraged will ultimately develop as tons as be an enterprising man or woman. On the alternative hand, a infant constantly snubbed and ridiculed will grow up doubting his competencies no matter how accurate they'll be in reality.

If what the others say to you can alternate the route of your future, then believe how what you tell your self each day is converting every gift 2d in your existence. Most of the time, however, this untapped strength of your communique with yourself is out of location. This is because of the fact, like a sponge, you absorb what the others have said to you and turn their memories into your memories. Of route, maximum of this takes location at a subconscious level but that does not advocate you can not reverse this unfavourable method. It is time you start changing the tales you inform yourself.

Switching Up the Self-communicate

Simply positioned, the testimonies you inform your self are called self-talk. These are the in fact uncensored, uncooked, spontaneous, and almost automatic mind that usually are on foot on a loop in your head. You can also ask, "These are just thoughts, what's the huge deal?" But the fact is that this self-speak does the rounds so regularly to your mind that those "just thoughts" end up the unconscious truths you swear your life with the resource of. It is while the ones truths come to be rigid to the element that they come to be an impediment to your development, which you recognize your thoughts is controlling you as opposed to the opportunity way round. So, all you genuinely need to do is exchange the script of your film. But how?

There is a manner that psychologists have used for years. It's known as "disputing". This is how it works.

Step 1: Sit in a non violent place and near your eyes. Bring into your recognition all the ones self-deprecating mind which you frequently discover yourself struggling with. It can be some element like, "I am this type of failure," or, "I need as a way to make absolutely everyone satisfied all the time," or maybe, "I will in no way very own a a success organization."

Step 2: Note down those mind as they're, with none modification. Sometimes, as you write the ones thoughts down you'll likely apprehend how irrational or perhaps silly some of the ones are. And yes, we frequently task ourselves to unrealistic irrational requirements. Regardless of the way they sound, phrase them down.

Step three: Objectively take a look at all of the statements you've got were given noted down. While doing this you can use positive guidelines like, "Is this logical?", "In my experience, how many instances can I think about which guide the statement and what number of refute it?", "When I use phrases like 'in no way' or 'constantly,' is that virtually accurate?", "Am I making any assumptions right here?" and "Am I wondering in simplistic black and white terms at the identical time as the reality can be more complex?" Note down your responses. This is on occasion additionally called Socratic Questioning. It is stated that Socrates ought to generally question his disciples assisting them flow into from superficial reasoning to a deep and extensive knowledge. Such Socratic Questioning also can assist discover the center notion pattern through way of stripping the argument of the irrational elements whilst stressful low-cost evidence for those distortions.

Step 4: Now that you have diagnosed the irrational statements and disputed them, the only difficulty left to do is update them with more healthy first-rate self-speak. For instance, "I am the shape of failure," may additionally need to get replaced through, "Failing at a assignment does no longer make me a failure. I am studying and failing permits me find out a higher way to be triumphant." Such reframing enables an person to show a perceived threat into an possibility that it virtually is.

Imagine for a 2d, how liberating it is probably to break the invisible shackles of your very non-public thoughts and ideals and flow at once to realise your potential the way you have been supposed to all along! Yes, that is the power that your thoughts have over you. And no jury can launch you from the jail of your mind. That you need to do all in your very very own.

The Unlimited Goodness Store

There is a store around the nook. It has the whole lot you have got were given were given favored, everything you can ever choice. Love, joy, peace. And sure, cash too. The most effective query is: Would you step out and walk in there? Would you select out up the cart and pass searching out happiness? Yes, it's far that easy. Except, the store isn't across the nook, it's inside you. And it's no longer a shop in any respect, it's the abundance mindset.

I recognize what you are thinking: I don't need this fluff. If all and sundry truely might also want to "appear" their very non-public happiness or even carry coins in their existence, we wouldn't have all this poverty and distress in lifestyles. You may be right to a point. It can not be denied that people are dwelling in much much less-than-ideal conditions everywhere in the international. But it is also essential to be conscious that most of this isn't so because of the natural scheme of factors, instead the systems that run our international. The political and financial systems are at a bonus at the same time as humans trust that they may't have sure matters and that advantageous political training and outstanding financial recommendations can deliver them what they don't have. Of direction, it might be silly to suggest that worldwide issues of peace and hunger can be solved thru converting mindset however it is able to virtually help whilst we remember character nicely-being.

As stated above, such a whole lot of millionaires and billionaires have come from quite humble backgrounds. Whether it's Oprah Winfrey or Laxmi Mittal, they are self-made people who select out to jump past their hurdles. An important factor of this transition is they cultivate a growth mind-set whilst most others from comparable backgrounds choose to exercise a hard and fast mindset. We communicate approximately this in detail in economic wreck three, however for now, permit's attempt to apprehend what this abundance mindset way.

There Is Enough for Everyone

One problem that humans regularly battle with on the path to success is sharing— sharing of popularity, electricity, resources, or maybe fulfillment itself. This struggle comes from the priority that within the occasion that they percent some thing comes to them, there might not be enough left for themselves.

Stephen Covey, the writer of the famous e-book The Seven Habits of Highly Effective People (2013), calls this a scarcity mentality. For those human beings, fulfillment is an problem of both their gain or others'. They can't envision a situation wherein they in addition to the others win. These human beings are continuously comparing and engaging in terrible competition with others which in the end hampers their increase. Rather than taking part with others, they pick to paintings by myself, believing that acknowledging others' achievement will by way of hook or with the aid of criminal amount to their failure. This mentality gives rise to a hoarding tendency which may additionally provide them fulfillment within the quick run but within the longer race, leaves them within the back of.

The abundance thoughts-set, alternatively, is the perception that there may be enough available for everybody. It works at the precept that now not all of us desires the identical subjects to be glad and therefore we don't need to compete for precis standards like achievement and reputation. It recognizes countless possibilities for collaborative increase and permits people pool of their assets to create a few thing larger and higher than one may create in my opinion.

Millionaires apprehend this reality perfectly nicely. Thus, for them, it isn't most effective approximately gathering wealth however collecting people. They realise that they cannot be successful on their very non-public, regardless of how gifted they'll be. They popularity on developing synergies that ensure achievement for all. They make actual contributions to humans's success, understanding entire nicely what goes around comes round. And most significantly, they prefer to see achievement as an final consequences of a collection try. They aren't in a rush to defeat humans in the race however typically bypass ahead on the issue in their people, right as much as the stop line.

Gratitude Will Keep You Afloat

When it consists of incorporating an abundance thoughts-set, gratitude performs a huge characteristic. Gratitude is all about appreciating what you have got rather than complaining about what you don't. Gratitude lets in you recognize that even within the worst of conditions, there may be nevertheless some aspect to be satisfied approximately. It helps you to see opportunities in preference to obstacles, opportunities in place of threats. There are multiple techniques that you may supply gratitude into your life.

One quite simple manner is to keep a "gratitude jar." Every day, you write on a piece of paper one element that makes you feel thankful. And you hold filling the jar. On a pre-decided day, or at the identical time as the jar is complete, or perhaps whilst you're having a awful day, you empty the jar and examine through the notes you have were given had been given written. It's a extremely good reminder that you are blessed. Another interest is to listing out 3 topics every day that make you sense thankful. You can phrase the ones in a journal and speak to it your gratitude mag. The more we educate our minds to look for the positives, the extra we're able to be open to receiving them at the identical time as our environments present them to us.

Most humans start out with extremely good zeal at the same time as doing those gratitude sports activities. They get glad and feel vitalized but regrettably, it dies down as unexpectedly because it had all commenced out. And the cause for that is they experience like as speedy due to the fact the novelty is out of place, the complete exercise turns into monotonous and almost mechanical.

The thing to recognize right here is gratitude is in no way stupid. If it feels that way you then clearly aren't doing it right. It is paramount that each time you do these sporting occasions, you do them as although it's the number one time. You allow the feeling of gratefulness run via your entire frame, experience that contentment strolling thru your veins. If eventually you experience like there was one component that you felt surely grateful for but can't consider various things, go along with that one problem. It's now not approximately checking bins however about feeling the abundance cradle your entire being.

Another detail that human beings war with is that many enjoy nearly chargeable for being content material material with what they have. It is sort of like if they are glad with what they've, they'll in no manner attempt to attain greater, in no manner do justice to their untapped capability. This couldn't be similarly from the fact. Gratitude has been, on numerous sports, validated to boom productivity, in my view in addition to organizationally.

There aren't any drawbacks to using gratitude whilst no longer the usage of it could have pretty a negative effect on our stylish well-being. This gratitude is prime to no longer only the way you feel however moreover what you create with the power of your focus.

Success Is Waiting for You

Positivity is cited so often but no longer frequently is it given any form. People let you realize to be extremely good all the time but no person bothers to talk about how. In this phase, we communicate approximately how you may result in the millionaire abundance mind-set for your lifestyles.

Step 1: Figuring Out What You Want

Simple sufficient? Sure feels so! You won't consider this but as smooth as this feels, maximum humans bungle up this number one stage quite badly. This isn't because of the reality they need incorrect subjects however because of the truth they need vague topics. They keep speakme about seeking to be wealthy. But you ask them wherein they see themselves in the next 12 months and that they draw a whole clean. You cannot make the equal mistake. The first actual step to appear an abundance of achievement to your life is to recognize what that success manner to you.

Detractors of the abundance mind-set frequently say that this is the stuff of fiction and fantasy. They bring about the aspect that if the abundance attitude honestly worked then honestly each person on the face of this earth could have a Ferrari! For them, everything is that belongings aren't in abundance and simply imagining they may be isn't going to help.

But right proper right here's what I suggest to them, and that is an check that you may do yourself too. Take any 10 human beings you understand and ask them one question—what does happiness and achievement imply to them? There's no manner that all of them will equate having a Ferrari with fulfillment and happiness. There's a possibility no longer even one character can also say it. And even though someone does, you'll furthermore locate nine extraordinary solutions which can be unique and severa.

The detail is, contrary to what we can be introduced as a whole lot as receive as true with, people find out pleasure in numerous things. It isn't always cash that brings them happiness but what cash can accomplish—a home in their very own, being able to spend extra time with their households, the liberty to do what they want, and so forth and so on. The crucial trouble to word right proper here is that money isn't the cause but the manner to a reason.

So, the question though stays, what's it which you need? What is the goal that your life is directed towards? You need to make it as unique as feasible. "Being rich" isn't always going to lessen it. Ask yourself the following questions when you have hassle narrowing it down:

1. Where do I see myself in the next six months or a three hundred and sixty five days or years?

2. What am I doing as quickly as I acquire my goal? What am I feeling?

3. What does this intention deliver to my life? How does it make a contribution to my happiness?

You can ask many greater such inquiries to yourself whilst setting the motive. The essential thing is to make it as actual for you as viable. Also, keep away from passing any judgments at this element— "There's no way this could ever get up!", "I might also need to never do that!", "This will in no way art work!". Keep them apart for just a few time, as we're able to deal with those within the later steps. For now, have a vision that remains proper to yourself. Many people even discover it useful to create a imaginative and prescient board. Visuals have the strength to seize our fancies like nothing else and imaginative and prescient forums have a propensity to make the precise use of those visuals. Let's say you need to adventure to Europe. Deck up your imaginative and prescient board with images of the locations you want to visit. Put a date whilst you would like to make that visit. Apart from placing your goals out into the universe, vision boards are also pretty a laugh to create.

Step 2: Drawing Out a Strategy

Manifesting isn't always about believing the paranormal forces will take over and shipping you in your reason. Rather, it's approximately making your thoughts do not forget in each viable way that you are in which you are presupposed to be. For this, it's far important to have a approach in order to take you on your motive.

Planning a way in your purpose can be masses greater simplified while you use S.M.A.R.T. Goals. S is for particular. We have already finished this in our first step. The next step is to make the ones dreams measurable (M). This manner that every time viable, have a quantitative discern assigned to the purpose. Rather than pronouncing, "I need to earn a incredible earnings," say a few factor like, "I need to earn $1,000 in earnings." Having a measurable cause will make it possible to track your development loads better.

After this, comes the workable (A) trouble. Devise a sensible goal. When walking in the direction of positivity, many people cross overboard with unrealistic desires.

For instance, whilst one has $50 in their account, to have a intention of having 1,000,000 dollars through the usage of the save you of the week might be a stretch. So, how about we begin with $500? Remember that you need to surely consider this can show up for it to art work.

Next, make this purpose relevant (R) to you. To bypass lower returned to the Ferrari instance, having a purpose without a doubt because of peer pressure doesn't paintings. Pick a purpose as a way to make you revel in actually fulfilled.

And in the end, make it time-certain (T). This is to say, dreams with out a timeline don't work. Let's say, you want to turn out to be a millionaire, but whilst? Now? Tomorrow? Next three hundred and sixty five days? Next lifetime? Having time-certain goals is the brilliant way to song your development. If you make a decision that you'll have the running facts of the percentage marketplace in the next month, at the give up of the month you can enforce steps if that intention has now not been reached.

Having a plan is of severe importance. Make certain you do your studies properly before diving in.

Step three: Getting the Necessary Skills

Millionaires don't take a seat round, looking for achievement to locate them. They take movement. They ensure they exit after a few issue it's miles they need and pull out all stops alongside the manner. There isn't always any substitute for talent. In these days's international, knowledge is your lifebuoy. So, do everything you can to hold your self up to date. Also, remember the more which you immerse your self in capability schooling, the more you're growing a simulation for your mind to agree with that the reason is certainly throughout the nook.

Join clubs, take courses, socialize with specialists from similar arenas. Be relentless. Know that information upgradation isn't truly an character exercising. The greater you surround your self with parents which can be suitable at what they do, the more you study. It takes a village to raise a little one? Well, it moreover takes a village to make a network of proficient, professional, and immoderate-aiming individuals who can develop together.

Optimizing your surroundings may additionally make some needs which are difficult in your relationships. But bear in mind: People who're unsupportive of your goals are weighing you down emotionally. If your desires are what subjects to you, you want to trim out the toxicity that effective human beings supply into your existence.

Step four: Working on Your Inner Self

As we've cited in the remaining economic spoil, jogging on yourself is probably the most crucial trouble you'll do. But it's moreover probable the maximum tough factor you'll do. It is less complicated to triumph over the outside obstacles but no longer the inner ones. There's a motive we are discussing it right here separately from what's already been mentioned formerly approximately beliefs and self-speak.

Most humans accept as real with that for us to take place fulfillment into our lives, we want to count on extremely good and best splendid thoughts. This isn't the case in any respect. Contrary to famous notion, the "positive millionaires" are very masses in touch with their lousy feelings too. They apprehend that denying horrible emotions is like telling you not to reflect onconsideration on a red elephant balancing a ball on its trunk even as standing on some different huge circus ball. Did you examine what happened there? You have been advised NOT to recollect it and that's precisely what you ended up doing! Most of the time, that is the same issue we do with those so-called poor emotions. We are so taken thru this desire to be effective that we expect the awesome manner to cope with horrible feelings is to close them out without a doubt.

The virtually a fulfillment people are able to experience their awful feelings with out judgments. They may be given the emotion, revel in it completely in that 2nd, and inside the method, let them cross in the end. On the other hand, folks that are constantly struggling towards the go with the flow in their emotions are overpowered with the aid of manner of the use of the pervasiveness in their unsightly emotions because of the fact those

Chapter 7: You Are Your Own Hero

When searching on the capacities of the human race as a whole, the possibilities are countless. But there may be one thing that people genuinely cannot do, it's miles sitting quite in containers. Most humans may want to agree it's a form of immoderate bodily torture to force a person to live internal a constrained box for too prolonged. But most human beings once in a while supply it any idea on the equal time as the bins are metaphors for the social expectations which we spend most of our lives looking for to in form into.

One such social gather is that of achievement and failure. We are too short to determine ourselves based at the actions we carry out. If we fulfill the expectations of society, get that fancy automobile, purchase that satisfactory home, have that properly-paying activity, we're a fulfillment. Otherwise, we are not. Well, the truth is lifestyles isn't that smooth. Rather than black or white, we are all sun shades of grey. This manner that absolutely everyone have perfect further to undesirable features and inclinations inside us. It is most effective through embracing each factors of ourselves, can we emerge as winners.

A Cherokee story is frequently heard ringing via the walls at the equal time as this self-embracing communication goes on:

The people story starts with an vintage grandfather giving his grandson an crucial lesson in existence. "Today, I am going to tell you approximately wolves. One is evil at the identical time because the alternative is ideal. They are every similarly strong. One can be your worst enemy and the opposite the satisfactory friend. They are constantly at battle, constantly preventing. And what's more, their battleground isn't a much-off forest. It's inner you. They stroll with you."

Concerned, the grandson asks cautiously, "So which wolf wins?"

The grandfather replies absolutely, "The one you feed, son. Always, the best you feed."

This story is a effective allegory that uncovers the power you have over your dark element. Remember, the wolves feed to your mind. The extra effective, kinder, inspiring thoughts you believe you studied, the stronger the brilliant wolf will become. The concept is not to eliminate the darkish aspect altogether till you're aiming for a halo on your head and wings in your lower back. No, the idea is to encompass every aspects of yourself and wield the power that comes from this interest.

Fixed Vs. Growth Mindset

The manner the evil wolf moves most customarily is thru essential us to recall what we're is what we'll ever be. This comes usually from our upbringing, now not only constrained to the circle of relatives we develop up in, however additionally the society and the culture we are a part of. Our flaws, our strengths, our capability—we're introduced as a good deal as trust that the ones will in no manner trade. Hence, every person who have become "fortunate sufficient" to accumulate the presents of multiple abilities and intelligence and capabilities, is certain to prevail, while the rest people are destined to trudge with the burden of our failed destinies.

What a cynical manner to stay isn't it? The truth, but, is quite the other. Think approximately it, if we absolutely have been so restrained in our functionality, what would be the thing of the education machine we've were given invested in globally, or the ever-increasing exchange and industries, or even the very nature of human civilizations which might be inclined closer to development and growth? And irrespective of this overwhelming proof, we nonetheless pick out out to bear in mind that just like the cereal inside the cardboard issue we ate this morning, we're certainly finite beings—not able to trade, not able to expand.

The actual news is there may be now a scientific cause for us to throw this mind-set inside the bin wherein it belongs. Carol Dweck, in her book Mindset (2006), talks notably about how a growth attitude is useful to humans at some point of professions, age corporations, and genders. She explores the general false impression that fulfillment simply takes area randomly to a select few talented humans. What others forget about approximately most usually is that people who upward thrust to achievement are those who have continued through problems, and innovated new techniques to challenges over the path in their gaining knowledge of curve.

The maximum splendid distinction that you could find out amongst a achievement millionaires and every body else is their fearless mind-set to life. Where each person else is cautious and shielding of themselves, the ones bold humans assignment into the unknown with the handiest cause of gaining knowledge of. It is due to this attitude that they're not threatened by way of a person else's intelligence or success however alternatively welcome it as an instance to look at from.

So, the query stays—how do you get there? Here are some matters you could consciously put into effect for your routine:

• Trash the consolation area: Not lots of what is going round on social media can be taken at face fee however there's a quote that does the rounds there this is as real as it is able to get: "Nothing correct ever comes out of consolation zones." So, step out of it right now. Do matters that make you uncomfortable. More mainly, do the topics that cause the "failure" alarm on your head. Take small steps, earlier than making the huge company jump, if you need to. Before going for the risky deal, make your self get at the dance ground if dancing makes you uncomfortable. The idea is to interrupt the dependancy of not doing subjects due to the truth you observed you will fail at them. Also, doing these gadgets and no longer getting the right end end result lets you apprehend that you could nonetheless stay to inform the story after the so-known as failing and that's no reason to prevent.

• Take duty: As we've noted earlier than, taking price of your future moreover manner which you take obligation for your actions. One very crucial issue that maximum humans miss is that taking responsibility isn't just like beating your self over matters. Taking obligation is ready figuring out what may be finished in another manner, learning the lesson and securing it in your toolkit for destiny use, and then moving on. People often overlook approximately the closing bit. So, next time you get some thing wrong and find your self attractive within the blame recreation, simply say "STOP" to yourself, get your self to recognize the extra suitable path of action, and as soon as the lesson is determined out, consciously have interaction your self with the similarly steps or some element else absolutely to distract your self.

• Keep expectations in test: It is our expectations of the consequences that greater regularly than not taint the entirety we do. It's nearly like we're so anxious to get to the holiday spot that we often miss out on the adventure altogether. Remind yourself every now and then to awareness at the motion instead of the final results. This might also additionally appear philosophical however whilst you aren't hung up on the outcomes, you will be loads more open to experimenting and innovating.

Working on the Strengths

We have talked loads approximately optimism and increase mind-set. An critical thing of every those attitudes is identifying your strengths. The unhappy reality is we belong to a society that highlights shortcomings way more than strengths. It is much less difficult to typecast a person as a failure in vicinity of respect the wealth of diverse strengths that they own. As cliche as it is able to seem, certainly everyone has unique strengths and also you owe it to yourself to end up privy to and nourish them.

I realise what you are wondering: But what if I don't recognize what my strengths are?! How would possibly I circulate approximately nourishing them then? Interestingly, four huge schooling of strengths were identified to make existence a tad an awful lot much less tough for you. These strengths have a unique significance in the administrative center but can also additionally even manual your information of your sturdy factors otherwise. It is vital to recollect, however, that the ones aren't person strengths but classes that might comprise multiple strengths within themselves.

The first class is the "envision" strength. The people with this strength in shape sincerely into manipulate roles. They have the functionality to look the massive image and continuously pass toward the aim. They are the ones who may additionally moreover have the most modern-day mind on the desk. They are occasionally so fast-paced with their thoughts that others discover it hard to preserve up with them. They are not afraid to undertaking out into the unknown and take a look at with stuff that no character has attempted out earlier than. They are those who've an pleasant mind-set which can be very contagious due to their sheer aura.

The subsequent magnificence is the "layout" strength. The human beings that belong to this category are analysts who're incredible at looking at the components that make up the big picture. They are super with information and count on in terms of precise goals and suggestions. They are fairly rational in their approach and prefer practicality over creativeness. They are prepared and feature a meticulous approach to the obligations that they undertake.

"Build" energy is the 0.33 category that includes folks that are fantastic at getting subjects performed. They successfully comply with instructions to constantly get the favored results. These human beings are able to artwork in a great deal much less-than-best conditions at the ground degree, however efficaciously pull off the duties although they're monotonous.

And ultimately, we've had been given the "operate" electricity. People who feature with this electricity are interested in the human element of the transactions. They are effective with human beings and own fantastic communication and negotiation competencies. They without a doubt have a spontaneity about them that helps them adapt to changing situations pretty efficiently on the same time as retaining the eye on the prize.

Where do you fall along those four dimensions? It is pretty feasible that you could have a mixture of extra than this sort of education. But preserve in mind that those lessons are only a guiding precept so you can apprehend wherein at the spectrum you stand. The growth mindset reminds us that none of these have impenetrable limitations. Think of them because the place to begin that lets in you to take off in preference to the ending places. There's not anything stopping you from obtaining the capability set from all or someone-of-a-type instructions.

Investing in Yourself

Learning new abilities or upgrading modern-day ones doesn't take vicinity through chance. It calls for dedication and a burning desire to gather extra than what you presently have. We may be speakme approximately the potential set specifically in detail inside the subsequent bankruptcy however allow's talk a bit about the mindset right here.

I even have visible too many people looking beforehand to greatness to unfold earlier than them. There isn't any planned attempt, no conscious try to get to that greatness. A commonplace excuse I pay interest all the time is, "I don't have any cash! How do you assume me to invest?!"

The fact is if you have the desire, you may locate strategies to squeeze coins out of your tight budget. Maybe make your coffee as opposed to dropping in at Starbucks, walk a few blocks as opposed to calling for a taxi. These little topics make a huge difference.

But what's even more important to understand is that investing in your self doesn't constantly ought to indicate more money, at least now not within the proportions that people regularly recall. Investing in yourself is set doing the little matters. It's no longer simplest about finding strategies to enhance yourself in phrases of expertise but moreover taking the time out to hobby for your bodily and emotional nicely-being.

• Keep Learning: Millionaires are constantly upgrading their information. They recognize that during a quick-changing international like ours, the best weapon that counts is relevant, up to date statistics. This is why they look at. According to investigate look at, a exceptional 80 5% of millionaires have a have a look at a median of one or books consistent with month, a few even more (Corley, 2009). Reading is one of the outstanding methods you can spend money on yourself.

• You are the excellent investment: What higher way to put money into yourself than in reality making an funding in yourself? Confused? I am speakme about a employer which you very own—put money into your private commercial organization. Get that dream off the floor. Save up, take loans, art work the greater hours. Do whatever it takes to very very own a commercial enterprise. You can't stay like a millionaire till you grow to be your very personal boss.

• Take some time out: It's actual that millionaires are relentless however they are additionally very acutely aware of their self-care exercises. They might also slog sixteen hours a day but once they take a damage, they will be capable of really unwind. Spend time in conjunction with your own family and pals that help you recharge emotionally.

Taking Advice with a Pinch of Salt

Another thing that I truly have seen harm too many dreams is the worry of what people will say if one fails. How usually have you had a superb idea that has in the end been snubbed with the useful resource of manner of people spherical you? Several instances, I actually have seen first rate innovation being tied down thru no longer practical but pretty pessimistic recommendation, in particular from people who very own no records inside the area. I am, of path, now not speakme approximately taking each concept that comes in your head and taking walks with it, however awful demotivating recommendation from human beings can make even the exquisite ideas lose steam right away.

But if it's far such awful recommendation, then why can we listen to it? Enter: the evil wolf. The horrible recommendation touches a nerve because it's far very just like what the evil wolf has been whispering in our heads all along. Think approximately this for an example. If a person calls a computer a typewriter, might also you trust them? No. What in the occasion that they vehemently argue with you over it? You'd although stay with your position. You'd very possibly discard their opinion as silly and ignorant. That's due to the fact you understand it's a computer, no longer a typewriter. But the instantaneous they may be pronouncing some aspect like, "Come out of your myth worldwide! You don't have sufficient cash to take this off the floor!" or "That idea isn't always something exquisite, I bet there are masses like that inside the marketplace!", you're taking their word for it. Why? Because it's like a confirmation of what the evil wolf has been pronouncing to you all this even as.

Don't get me incorrect, I am no longer announcing that everyone says those objects to deter you. They may properly be trying to protect you however bear in mind you are the one making the very last choice and you want to make the selection amongst staying protected or taking place hand and having a bet on your self. Put a aware filter in your mind to display out grievance. This does not mean you neglect approximately about it, in no way. Criticism can be a totally rich beneficial resource to your improvement. The filter out excellent manner that in vicinity of taking it at its face charge, you study it logically and objectively to discern out the remarks that could gain you and sieve out the relaxation.

The Whole Package

The one problem that millionaires have in commonplace with every other, other than the wealth, is their mind-set. Their idea strategies are impartial of what others anticipate because of the reality they care lots a great deal much less about becoming in and extra approximately achieving their imaginative and prescient with the aid of manner of creating modern paths of reaching it. This is, of path, no longer to say the key is to select the normal choice, but extra the selection because of this the maximum to themselves.

Another difficulty is that millionaires don't chase cash. Rather they favor to pick out excellence. They try to recollect how they may be capable of best what they may be contributing to the world. And this imaginative and prescient is what drives them more than the greed for money. It is due to this imaginative and prescient that those self-made millionaires can live to inform the tale the hardships. The founder of Oracle, Larry Ellison, for instance, is a traditional instance of the rags to riches story. He grew up in a slum at some stage in World War II and yet controlled to build up billions in internet nicely truely well worth at the same time as he retired. Oprah Winfrey is every other shining instance of techniques a existence riddled with poverty and abuse can end up a millionaire life with recognition and popularity simplest because of a imaginative and prescient in the course of which she strived and strived.

Now that we have had been given identified the gaps in our emotional and attitudinal processing that require a few brilliant-tuning, it is time to transport at once to the bigger elements of man or woman that would require a few artwork, each in the manner you seem to others in addition to the way you engage with them. In this monetary disaster, we deal with the life talents which may be unnoticed all too often at the same time as carving the route to success.

The Million Dollar Problem

If there's one issue that all self-made millionaires are then it's that they'll be all hassle-solvers. They come to be privy to a hassle and cross after perfecting the approaches to treatment that trouble. Now, those problems may not usually be issues going via humanity however via issues, I advise areas that each have scope for reinforcing comfort for current stakeholders or ones that provide sufficient opportunity for innovation to create new stakeholders. Millionaires don't sit down down around moping and cribbing approximately how the area is a tough place. They pick out to artwork in processes that change that reality. Take Elon Musk, as an example. He recognized the trouble of pollutants and the large carbon footprint that our automobiles were leaving and launched the electric car opportunity inside the form of Tesla Motors.

This problem-solving capability has masses to do with their success. But wherein does it come from and how are you going to emulate it in your course to success? In his precept of psychosocial improvement, Erik Erikson talks approximately the improvement of the only-of-a-type function of competency during the "Industry vs. Inferiority" diploma someplace some of the age of 5 and thirteen years. Yes, that early! Essentially, he talks approximately how human beings float from one diploma to any other, and counting on whether or not or not or not the ones ranges are successfully resolved or not, they increase both virtues or pathologies. So, on this precise degree, if given the right encouragement and opportunity to cope with their issues, children exhibit a sturdy feel of competence and regularly showcase the "I can do it!" thoughts-set. This is an crucial mindset to have even as looking to solve a problem—the perception that you could nonetheless make a distinction to at least one's surroundings. And irrespective of whether or not you had been for the purpose that opportunity and encouragement for your teenagers, you could alternate that now.

The first step to turning into a problem solver is actively wondering the subjects in the environment in region of passively accepting them. It is most effective this in no way-ending interest that can help you recognize a hassle. Another crucial detail on the identical time as identifying those issues is if you want to peer them objectively as information and no longer as projected critiques. When you're figuring out the trouble, additionally recognize the cause which you need to get at. You don't need to reflect onconsideration on how you can benefit it but, handiest understand what it is you want. This is some component millionaires are frequently placed doing. Even even though they'll haven't any clue as to how they'll get there, they're genuinely certain in which they need to reach.

Then comes the extent of brainstorming. This is all about thoughts. Remember to not shoot down your thoughts just yet on the idea of practicality or feasibility. Let each idea be positioned on the desk. The reason for this is maximum of the time, we have a tendency to evaluate our thoughts even earlier than they are honestly fashioned, therefore losing out on possibilities. Also gunning down the ideas in advance may be very possibly to create a mental block or a bias in competition to your very own capability, every of which can be the worst enemies of critical wondering.

Once these thoughts take form, now it's time for that assessment which you have been so eager to engage in. At this thing, anticipate significantly about how possible it's far and approximately the possible results. Keep up the assessment and evaluation method until there may be first-rate one left. This is your idea that you must be on foot with. It is in this segment which you'll do your studies and can even ask for feedback from humans, and not simply one or people but have a larger, extra numerous, and extra knowledgeable sample to attract your stop from.

And the very last step is the execution of the concept. This is in which maximum humans get cold toes because of the fact that is wherein the idea starts getting actual in phrases of investment of some time, effort, and coins. If it's far an innovative product, as an instance, then it's miles probably to go through a number of trial and mistakes. Most a fulfillment marketers have been via the ones levels of frustration and helplessness, and have emerged on the other aspect that hundreds wiser. The tale of Thomas Edison and his invention of the lightbulb is a traditional example. It is also essential to undergo in mind that to get to the lightbulb, Edison moreover needed to reinvent diverse of things along the way. Self-made millionaires have patience, patience, and the belief in their thoughts that maintains them going. An important sub-step proper right here is to be open to the commands. Learning from the errors at this degree is one of the topics that strongly fuels further development.

An related capacity that has maximum humans flummoxed is the choice-making manner. I regularly listen people asking the query, "How do I make the incredible choice?" The truth is there's no machine. Of route, you can employ techniques which encompass purpose evaluation of the professionals and cons, or developing a hierarchy of alternatives from the maximum to the least perfect. But even after this, there may be no guarantee that the choice will turn out exactly the manner you planned. This is wherein your adaptability comes into the photograph. Hoping for the fine and making geared up for the worst, greater or tons a whole lot much less, sums up this situation. It is vital to no longer lose your reputation after you have had been given been thrown off-direction by means of the usage of an unexpected aspect. The most vital element, however, is virtually you make a decision after your preliminary evaluation. I absolutely have visible too many opportunities out of place due to the fact the man or woman certainly did not make the choice at the proper time. And be privy to how I emphasize the proper time in choice to the "right" preference.

Communication Is the Word

If you accept as true with billionaire Richard Branson, conversation is the maximum vital capability you'll collect on the street to fulfillment. As referred to earlier than, millionaires don't get there all with the useful resource of themselves. They have their people to fall once more on. We find out the ones relationships in more detail later however it's far essential to phrase right right here that those relationships have conversation at their middle. Whether it's in near relationships or their business interactions, millionaires get their conversation capabilities proper on element.

The largest mistake humans make while communicating is believing that they have interplay with others only through the terms they will be announcing. This couldn't be farther from the truth. In fact, non-verbal cues absorb everywhere amongst 70 to ninety three% of the conversation (Advaney, 2017). There are incredible variations within the claimed percentage but even though we take the pessimistic figures, that is a pretty large chunk. It is those non-verbal cues that could make or wreck your conversation with others. Several self-made millionaires warn toward the risks of ignoring the energy of body language. Your facial expressions, even the manner in which you stand, and the entirety in amongst, it's far vital to do what those millionaires do to get the basics right.

1. The handshake: Barbara Corcoran, the founding father of The Corcoran Group, believes the handshake to be one of the figuring out elements in whether or now not she trusts a person or no longer. A unfastened, misplaced, and sweaty handshake can break your first have an impact on. On the opportunity hand, a organisation handshake symptoms self assurance and fact this is absolutely assuring to the alternative man or woman in any interplay.

2. Eye contact: Another mistake that people make is fending off eye contact, searching across the room while a person is talking with you, looking down, blinking too much—those all constitute an nearly suspicious behavior. On the alternative of the spectrum, there are also folks who stare; their eye contact may be a touch intimidating. Either way, no brownie factors for guessing it's now not doing

masses unique for the connection that is being hooked up.

three. Impatience: One of the golden rules of conversation is, "Listen in advance than you communicate." Listening actively together together with your entire body permits amplify a right away connection with the speaker. Basic gestures like nodding (no longer overly enthusiastically in spite of the fact that) or utterances like "Hmmm" pass an prolonged manner on this regard. Also, looking at your watch, interrupting, or getting fidgety even as the alternative character is speakme, are a specific no-no.

four. The high-quality line amongst self perception and conceitedness: I clearly have seen severa people drift that one. Jay Leno, the famous former host of The Tonight Show, makes a sturdy case for kindness within the smallest interactions. Being assured is the excellent but being too cocky approximately it in no way does some thing properly for everyone. So, make certain to exhibit all your strengths but additionally to do it humbly.

5. Jargon: Too many people, of their zeal to show off their knowledge, make their pitches overstuffed with jargon. This is a catastrophe equipped to arise because of the truth no longer all understand the technicalities. Rather than the ones human beings coming across as clever, they come upon as understand-it-all brats who couldn't be to make the information greater palatable for the hundreds.

6. No idea to the "brand:" You are your very own logo. All your movements, perceptions, or even social media presence boom to an photo. This photograph precedes you in most of your interactions. The art work is to make all of these cohesive. It is also important to apprehend each time you communicate with a few other person, you're each making them like your brand and choose it over again in the destiny or making them need to neglect about approximately approximately you virtually.

Besides those, you glaringly want to study your tone of voice, your posture, and your body orientation whilst speaking. Having an open posture in which you are going via the individual that is speaking is constantly suitable.

But having said all of that, you don't get to the million mark via being timid and restricted. It is important to talk your mind assertively. Many people get this wrong due to the truth their regular fashion of communique is one of the extremes, each competitive or passive. They experience almost backed proper into a nook the instantaneous the verbal exchange goes off their intellectual script. The surrender end end result? Same as a cat could react, they pounce not out of bravery however nearly out of fear. The different immoderate is, of route, wherein they preserve piling it on till in some unspecified time within the destiny the lid inevitably blows off. The ethical of the story is, for assertive conversation to occur, feelings want to be tackled effectively.

The Best Kind of Intelligence

Elle Kaplan, the CEO and founding companion of LexION Capital, swears with the useful resource of the importance of emotional intelligence on your journey to success. Science has the identical opinion with Kaplan. The researcher Daniel Goleman even is going a step further, pronouncing emotional intelligence or emotional quotient (EQ) is probably an lousy lot extra crucial than intelligence quotient (IQ). In his book Emotional Intelligence (1995), he goes on to define five components of EQ that is probably useful to our present dialogue.

1. Self-recognition: This talks about the amount to which the man or woman is aware of their very personal emotions, strengths, and weaknesses. This self-attention lets in them to take feedback in a high quality way in preference to taking it too in my view or ignoring it altogether. This moreover consists of the attention approximately how their movements and terms impact others.

2. Self-regulation: Self-interest leads the man or woman lightly into self-law in which as they recognise the effect they have got on others, moreover they behave with extra restraint and strength of mind.

three. Motivation: People with immoderate EQ are pushed with the resource in their ambition and desire to gain. They show off a hopeful disposition and are much more likely than others to get better from undesirable situations. These human beings don't require outside motivators but can intrinsically encourage themselves to attain better.

four. Empathy: The capability to understand others' emotions and connect to them on a deeper degree is drastically important. They are able to placed themselves in others' footwear and empathize with what the other man or woman may be feeling. This allows them be extra compassionate in their interactions.

five. Social talents: An character with excessive EQ is extremely good with human beings. They are able to form actual, deep connections primarily based on compassion and recollect. Their relationships are often characterized via a robust experience of mutual admire and extra prolonged-term in desire to certainly quick-term and opportunistic.

Now, you could say all that sounds outstanding however the "how" query although remains. You'd be happy to have a look at no character is born with emotional intelligence. Have you seen babies who're in exceptional manipulate of their emotions? I is probably appreciably concerned if you respond with a "positive" to that query. So, no. No one is born with it and in the long run arguments like "They are actually gifted," or "They are so lucky," can take a hike for now. EQ is a few element you expand with staying power and electricity of mind. Here are some subjects you could do.

Step 1: Examine your pattern of behaviors. Critically have a look at some past instances you may take into account. See if you were overly competitive, or simply passive, or maybe passive-competitive with sarcastic feedback. Once you've got those styles discovered, remind your self each every now and then, you have got were given a preference to act otherwise. You are not the scared cat in the corner. You ought to stand your floor guilt-loose. It is vital to get the steadiness proper. It received't show up in the first flow. Beliefs and behaviors that have solidified over such a number of years don't melt in an afternoon however preserve at it and you may experience the alternate.

Step 2: The above-stated patterns come specifically from assumptions. You can also moreover assume that the opportunity person is suppressing you whilst they will handiest be expressing their very private opinion. This assumption fast becomes a conclusion and due to this the thoughts goes into autopilot. You save you investigating similarly due to the fact "you without a doubt apprehend it." This step is prepared delaying the autopilot for as long as possible. If you have got a take a look at extra younger children, you may find they're in no way on autopilot. They are continuously curious, constantly asking instead of assuming. This dependancy of curious questioning is a few issue adults must in reality have a study from children.

Step three: Now it's time to deliver that empathy into motion. Prioritize listening in desire to speakme. Try and note the emotions inside the returned of the words, even body language may additionally moreover offer vital cues in this regard. But that's not all there may be to empathy. Empathy also can moreover require which you replicate every other's vulnerability with the useful resource of a few diploma of self-disclosure as prolonged as it does not direct the point of interest faraway from the opportunity man or woman's narrative. This shows them that it's good enough to be much less than best.

Step four: Now that the self and different reputation is looked after, allow's flow into to the issue that humans find out the hardest—staying inspired. First and most important, make certain that extrinsic motivating factors like cash, grades, popularity lose their luster after some time however the intrinsic motivational flame maintains burning. Thus, it's miles crucial to find what you are honestly captivated with. We talk this more in bankruptcy 6 but for now, it would suffice to mention that the satisfactory way you'll ever prevent procrastinating is whilst you discover some aspect that does not will allow you to rest till it's finished. All self-made millionaires file this restlessness. But how soon you find out that aspect is based upon upon the amount of strive you install right now.

The Millionaire Look

All that we've got got got discussed up to now is ready the inner working of the millionaire mind. Now we talk approximately letting that super personality shine via the way you appear to others. The significance of first impressions can not be pressured sufficient. And you need to make yours now not whatever a good deal much less memorable. But please don't misread this to intend you want to put on flashy garments and present day day sun sunglasses and cool devices. You'd do higher now not to fashion yourself with any of those. But being groomed is crucial. A easy look is expert; a messy look isn't. You need to admit, it's hard to take someone seriously whilst they may be sporting shabby Bermuda shorts and feature raveled hair.

This does no longer suggest at all which you only want to place on stupid formals all of the time. The essential component at the same time as dressing for achievement is to find a balance amongst being your self, being unforgettable, and the usage of domestic the proper branding message. Millionaires don't usually placed on fits in recent times. They find out a material cabinet that makes them revel in snug and elegant. Whether it's T-shirts and denims or fits, be aware about the emblem that you are. Remember that each one the messaging you do desires to be coherent. It is only at the same time as your emblem has consistency and is continuously reinforced through your interactions, will you be etched in people's memory.

Some millionaires remember you want to invest in handsome footwear and luggage at the same time as others have a extra minimalistic method. Regardless of which aspect you come back down on, consider that the maximum essential factor is to take the time that may be visible thru the alternative party. This lets in them to recognise you are intense approximately the interplay with them. But irrespective of what you placed on, be aware that your records and your sincere transparency can be your incredible accessory.

Chapter 8: Mornings To Mega-Mornings

It isn't any mystery that mornings hold top notch functionality to now not only make your day however moreover to exchange your worldview. But it is also proper that human beings find out themselves trapped in awful-day cycles, most of that have their roots inside the identical immoderate-functionality mornings. Think of a mean morning for your existence. These might also range notably primarily based definitely totally on whether you stay on my own or have a family. Regardless of your state of affairs, however, you can possibly relate thoroughly to the morning madness that we discuss with.

If you have got were given were given youngsters, you most probably spend a massive amount of time screaming until you're hoarse, trying to get them equipped for university. And all this at the identical time as you yourself are becoming ready for paintings. If you're single, mornings, in which you have were given overslept and are consequently past due, aren't too rare. The truth is on the identical time due to the fact the relaxation people warfare to get our mornings in form, millionaires have already pocketed the victories a good manner to force them via the relaxation of their excessive-powered day. A have a look at via manner of OnePoll and Thermador, cited inside the New York Post, determined that in 3 contributors wanted they had more manage over their mornings. If mornings can simply be that impactful, then having a green morning routine is essential to a healthful in addition to a rich way of existence.

Becoming a Morning Person

Some millionaires report being up and about through spherical 5 in the morning at the same time as others start their mornings even earlier thru 4.30 a.M. On the possibility hand, the facts from The Sleep Cycle app claims that a mean

American wakes up at 7 a.M. (Thomas, 2019). That's and a 1/2 of hours misplaced proper there. But maximum folks would possibly agree that, but lots we strive to place a extremely good spin on putting the alarm clock for four.30 a.M., not everybody experience inspired by means of manner of the use of the concept. Have you ever idea about why this could be? The maximum commonplace solution to that is, "There is not any way my sleep might be whole with the resource of 4.30 a.M. That's a tad too close to the time I visit mattress."

While most enjoy they are slaves to their organic clock and certainly are not morning humans inherently, the fact is one in each of a type. The truth is your natural clock runs on the time you region, it's not the other way round. If you sense your sleep received't be complete then you definitely clearly have the electricity to reset your clock. It also can take the time but your body is a lot extra adaptable than you consider you studied. If this wasn't the case then how have to one ever go with the flow to a metropolis in a one-of-a-type time region? Wouldn't they be jet-lagged for the relaxation of their lives? The thing is the declare "I am a night time owl" or "I am a morning person" is a fable.

It's time to reset your clock to offer you a head begin on your days. Here's how you could get commenced:

1. Make high-quality you get a amazing night time's sleep. Being a morning person isn't about waking up groggy after slumbering best four hours. If you're a "mild" sleeper who wakes up with every little sound, optimize your environment for the least viable disturbances. Use earplugs if you have to, but bear in mind the remarkable of sleep is honestly as vital as the amount.

If you are the so-called "insomniac" who cannot sleep, attempt taking a heat water bathtub to lighten up your muscle mass proper before you get to bed. Breathing-targeted meditation may additionally moreover help loosen up you similarly. The idea is to now not get traumatic about the decided sleep time and hours of sleep but to recognition on letting your body relax as a whole lot as viable, contributing to the regeneration technique.

2. Drawing a nap agenda is crucial. Avoid drastic fluctuations in sleep times as a protracted manner as viable. But moreover, don't be so inflexible approximately it, that it offers you no leeway to do whatever else. Sleep is a calming, soothing hobby and that's the way it have to live.

3. Make high exceptional that the room you sleep in has sufficient natural mild coming sooner or later of the day. This way your body receives a higher hazard to reply to the growing solar via secreting lesser and lesser melatonin, as a result making your transition into the day a whole lot more gradual and remarkable.

four. And probable the most vital, positioned your smartphone away at the least 1/2 of an hour in advance than you get to mattress. The blue mild on your mobile phone does exactly the opposite of putting you to sleep, instead it increases alertness and consequences in dry eyes which might also hamper your sleep similarly. Also, the steady notifications thru the night time time are likely to lessen your REM sleep, that's vital to the method of recuperation.

Most those who make the transition to "a morning character" tend to be pretty miserable within the starting. But as they begin experiencing the advantages of an splendid sleep time table, they frequently marvel why they didn't do it in advance. It is important to look this not as an imposed retribution but as a brilliant possibility to move in the route of your aim with more electricity. Vince Stanzione, in his ebook The Millionaire Dropout (2013), offers a splendid angle on beginning the day early. He proposes that through waking simplest an hour earlier, you may nearly create a in addition day of seven hours. To all individuals who bitch of no longer getting sufficient time, this appears like a notable deal, doesn't it?

The Routine That's Not-So-Routine

Establishing a morning recurring may additionally appear to be a big assignment but when you get into the rhythm of it, you'll find out that it's no longer simplest smooth but moreover distinctly rejuvenating. It is decided that successful people divide their routines into more or less three regions which is probably most essential to their well-being—searching after themselves, nurturing the relationships with their cherished ones, and strategically making plans for their careers.

The Mental Workout

Self-care is a few detail you do to keep and enhance your fitness. This is a trending problem count presently all-over social media and rightly so. But frequently people have a propensity to misunderstand self-care to intend doing a little factor fun. Though self-care in its actual experience does experience appealing, it can not continuously revel in so inside the 2d. I actually have encounter many individuals who discover meditation uninteresting and suppose workout is too much paintings. Though those might also feel especially tough within the first few days, the human frame has a way of adapting to useful subjects with greater readiness than we credit score it for.

So, wherein do you begin? By channeling your inherent power that we mentioned within the preceding chapters. Three techniques had been showed to have the only results—meditation, visualization, and confirmation.

Meditation

When it involves meditation, it's miles important to bear in mind some things. Firstly, in this territory, you're the boss. The final results is based upon surely on you. While that might be a touch intimidating, it's also comforting because of the truth considering the fact that it's far independent of out of doors elements, it approach you get to exercise most manage over the state of affairs. Secondly, you may do meditation at the same time as you're doing whatever at all. The dated concept that you need to sit nonetheless in one area while doing it would seem a chunk unnatural to 3 people. For those, I say taking a walk additionally can be a meditation in case you do it the right manner. Lastly, the best rule at the equal time as meditating is to be within the 2d, and to continuously deliver yourself another time from all of the places your thoughts wanders.

Such aware meditation can be especially useful in handling pressure, in trying to disconnect with the out of doors global and forging an inner connection, and most importantly, in knowing that your "self" is break away all which you do. This cements an identity this is indifferent from the final results however is engaged inside the present 2d of doing.

You can soak up meditation in lots of unique procedures. Some pick counting breaths as a focusing mechanism, others want to have interaction in chanting sounds and mantras like "Oum" to channel their electricity at the same time as however others may also choose to play an device, virtually immersed in the gift 2d of that experience. What makes meditation impactful is the understanding that you could calm the chaotic hurricane interior you and no matter the state of affairs outdoor, all you need to do for it's far breathe. It does not depend quantity what you do this takes you there but what's more important is consistency. Even 10 minutes of meditation every day can garner extensive blessings for you.

Visualization

Though visualization may be considered to be a subcategory of the meditation exercising, it nonetheless wins a separate spot in our communicate for the sheer energy that it includes inside itself. While meditation is ready appealing your conscious self, visualizations have plenty to do in conjunction with your unconscious mind. Before you discard this as fictional fluff, preserve in mind this: Can you located quite a few on the amount of statistics you gadget each day? Most likely not.

The human mind is pervasively overloaded with stimulation. If your conscious thoughts spent time processing every and each stimulus, it'd probably fry your mind right away. Thus, what the mind does is it creates chunks of records in location of setting it one at a time as impartial gadgets. For example, whilst you exit you might see motorcycles and cars and wood and houses. If you needed to approach each bike, car, tree, and building one by one, that would power you loopy, but because you've got got already were given your neat categories, you can simply place the incoming facts inside the ones classes, and you're taken care of.

That is wherein your subconscious mind is to be had in. It stores all this information and directs your subconscious mind without overwhelming it. But all of us recognize that our unconscious minds can be very well wrong. As is pretty obvious within the prejudices and stereotypes we hold, the types the facts goes into might not be accurate in any respect. And the ones defective representations might be about our private self as thousands as others. Until and besides our representation of ourselves in our aware and subconscious mind isn't aligned with each notable, we're able to constantly discover ourselves conflicted on our direction to fulfillment.

Visualization allows us align those images. I am not proper proper right here to inform you which you visualize some aspect and it magically seems in the the front of you. But while you visualize yourself in a way that's now not in keeping with your aware self, your unconscious mind may be very possibly going to sabotage all of your tries to get there. Hence, it's far critical to give your self-photograph a effective spin and visualization lets in with exactly that.

www.ingramcontent.com/pod-product-compliance
Lightning Source LLC
Chambersburg PA
CBHW070556010526
44118CB00012B/1339